Canadian Living

150 ESSENTIAL
BEEF, PORK & LAMB RECIPES

BY THE CANADIAN LIVING TEST KITCHEN

Transcontinental Books

EDITOR'S NOTE

IT DOESN'T SEEM TO MATTER what time it is in The Test Kitchen – the time is always right to dig in to a juicy, tender steak. Sure, we all love our vegetables (and, really, who doesn't love starch?), but the food specialists at *Canadian Living* are all self-proclaimed carnivores. As we were growing up, meat was always the foundation on which our meals were built.

Today I eat a little less meat than I used to, serve it in smaller portions and choose a variety of local, ethically raised cuts, from snout to tail. I also savour meat more. I'm more thoughtful about where my food comes from now than I ever was as a kid. But meat still has a very important place in my diet and the food I cook for my family, as it does for so many Canadians.

As a nation, we love red meat. Many of our traditional dishes, both native to Canada and derived from our diverse ethnic influences, are based on three basic hearty meats: beef, pork and lamb – and sometimes more than one. (Think tourtière!)

It helps that there are so many different ways to enjoy those three fundamental ingredients. From thick-cut chops to juicy burgers to fall-off-the-bone braises to roasts dripping with velvety sauces, there are countless dinner options to dream up every night – no matter what time of year, how special the occasion or what your budget allows. And now with 150 more recipes in your repertoire, you should never run out of delicious inspiration.

Eat well!

– Annabelle Waugh,
Food director

150
ESSENTIAL
**BEEF,
PORK
& LAMB
RECIPES**

74

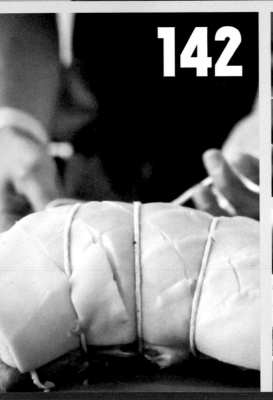

16

142

8

204

CONTENTS

1

MEAT CUTS

CONTENTS

10

BEEF
Premium Cuts
Economical Cuts
Versatile Cuts

12

PORK
Premium Cuts
Economical Cuts

14

LAMB
Premium Cuts
Economical Cuts
Versatile Cuts

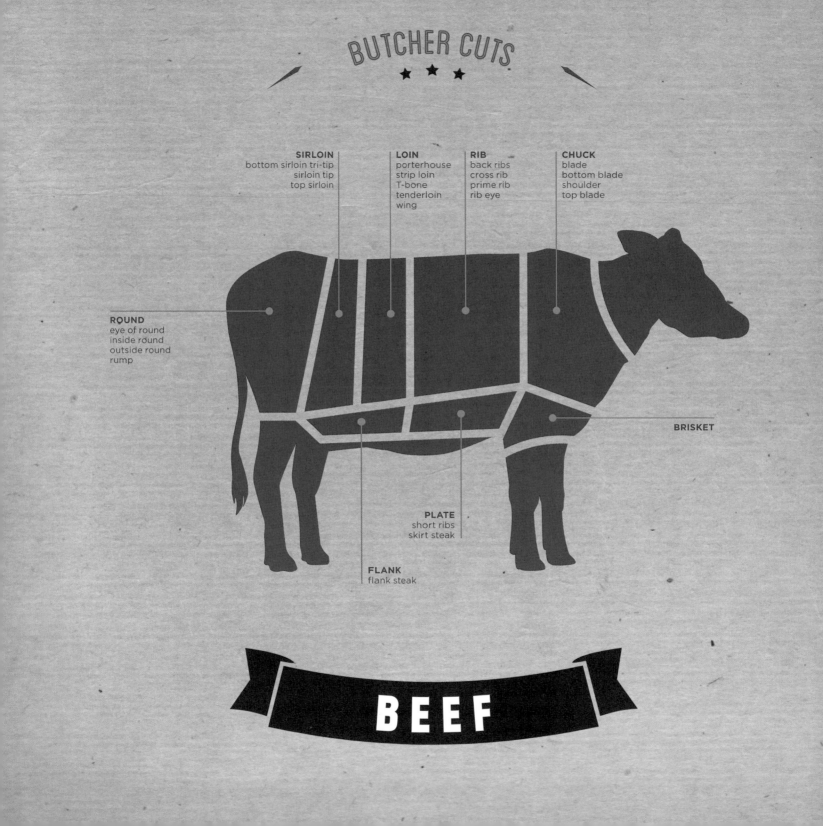

BEEF

PREMIUM CUTS

PREMIUM OVEN ROASTS

➡ prime rib (rib roast, standing rib roast)
  rib eye
  strip loin
  tenderloin (Chateaubriand)
  top sirloin
  wing

Premium oven roasts are cut from the loin, rib and sirloin sections. They have a covering of fat and more marbling than other cuts, which produces a more tender roast. There are also mini versions of some of these cuts that total less than 1 lb (450 g) and are designed to cook up quickly for smaller families. You'll also find rotisserie versions of these roasts, which are cut specifically to cook evenly on a spit over the barbecue.

GRILLING STEAKS

➡ porterhouse
  rib eye (Delmonico, if boneless)
  strip loin (entrecôte, New York)
  T-bone
  tenderloin
  top sirloin

Premium grilling steaks are cut from the loin, sirloin and rib sections. The loin can be cut two ways: by removing the tenderloin and strip loin separately, or cutting steaks that contain portions of both the tenderloin and the strip loin (T-bone and porterhouse). Tender grilling steaks can be cooked with minimal preparation. Cook leaner steaks, such as tenderloin, to medium-rare to keep them juicy and succulent.

ECONOMICAL CUTS

OVEN ROASTS

➡ bottom sirloin tri-tip
  inside round
  outside round
  rump/heel of round (rump roast)
  sirloin tip

Regular oven roasts are cut from the hip and loin sections. They are less tender and marbled than premium oven roasts, but marinating them for four to 24 hours does a great job of tenderizing them. There are mini and rotisserie versions of these cuts too.

POT ROASTS

➡ blade
  bottom blade (boneless)
  brisket
  cross rib
  shoulder
  top blade

Cut from the tougher chuck and brisket sections, pot roasts need to be cooked using a moist heat technique, such as braising, slow cooking or pot roasting. It takes a long time to tenderize these cuts, so they're always cooked until well done and almost falling-apart tender.

MARINATING STEAKS

➡ flank steak
  skirt steak

These steaks are cut from the flank and plate (front portion of the belly) sections. Less tender than grilling steaks, they benefit from standing in an acidic-based mixture for four to 24 hours to tenderize them. Marinating steaks should be grilled only to medium-rare or medium: Anything beyond that tends to produce tough meat.

VERSATILE CUTS

GRILLING & BRAISING CUTS

➡ back ribs
  eye of round
  flank steak
  short ribs

Eye of round, cut from the hip, and flank steak, cut from the back of the belly, are both suited to a variety of cooking methods and benefit from marinades and rubs. If grilling or roasting, cook them to no more than medium-rare to prevent tough, dry meat. The same applies to grilling. Cut thin slices (across the grain for flank steak) for the most toothsome results. Back ribs, cut from the rib section, and short ribs, cut from the plate section, are delicious braised or grilled. Both cuts are well marbled and become meltingly tender when cooked for a long time.

DONENESS TEMPERATURES

Oven roasts are best cooked rare to medium; however, premium roasts can be cooked to well done and still be tender thanks to better fat marbling. Steak doneness is definitely a matter of taste. For consistency, use an instant-read thermometer to judge – cutting into steaks to check causes all those delicious juices to leak out. For medium-rare, cook to 145°F (63°C); for medium, to 160°F (71°C); for medium-well, to 165°F (74°C); and for well-done, to 170°F (77°C). For ground beef, always ensure the internal temperature reaches 160°F (71°C) to kill any harmful bacteria.

PORK

PREMIUM CUTS

LOIN CUTS

➠ baby back ribs
butterfly chop (boneless)
loin chop (bone-in or boneless)
loin roast (bone-in or boneless)
peameal bacon
sirloin roast
sirloin steak
tenderloin

The loin, located on the back, is the most tender and expensive part of the pig. Attached to it are the back ribs and tenderloin. Once these are removed, the remaining muscle is divided into three parts: the rib, or blade (closest to the shoulder); the centre cut; and the sirloin end (closest to the leg). The loin is tender and lean; it is best cooked by dry high heat, such as roasting, grilling or pan-frying.

ECONOMICAL CUTS

SHOULDER CUTS

➠ picnic shoulder roast
shoulder blade chop
shoulder blade roast
shoulder butt roast
stewing cubes

A shoulder cut contains the highest level of fat, making it ideal for sausages and slow braising. It consists of two parts: the blade (butt) portion (closest to the loin), which is tender enough for dry roasting and fatty enough for braising, and the picnic portion, which is often made into chops or ground.

LEG CUTS

➠ cutlet (schnitzel)
ham (fresh, smoked, bone-in or boneless)

The plump hind leg, or ham, is smoked, cured (for prosciutto) or sliced into luncheon meat. It is usually sold whole or cut into three sections: the inside, the outside and the tip. Ham is lean, so it is best cooked by dry heat, such as roasting or pan-frying.

BELLY & VARIETY CUTS

➠ belly (fresh, cured or smoked as bacon)
foot
hock
spareribs
tail

The belly includes side ribs, from which spareribs are cut, as well as side bacon, pancetta (Italian-style bacon) and salt pork.

DONENESS TEMPERATURES

Pork is done when it's still juicy and has a hint of pink in the middle, or when an instant-read thermometer inserted in the thickest part reads 160°F (71°C). You can remove roasts from the oven when they reach 155°F (68°C) and tent them with foil. Let them stand for 10 minutes or more to come up to 160°F (71°C). Ground pork should always be cooked to 160°F (71°C).

BUTCHER CUTS
★ ★ ★

LOIN
double loin chop
loin chop
loin roast
tenderloin
top loin chop

RIB
crown roast
rack
rib chop
rib roast

SHOULDER
neck
shoulder chop
shoulder roast
stewing cubes

LEG
butterflied leg roast
centre leg roast
leg chop
leg steak
shank
short cut leg
sirloin roast
whole leg

FORESHANK
foreshank
riblets
rolled roast
spareribs

BREAST
ground breast
sausage

LAMB

LAMB

PREMIUM CUTS

RIB CUTS

➠ crown roast
  rack
  rib chop
  rib roast

The rib area is tender and flavourful, with an outer layer of fat that (if not trimmed off) melts and bastes the meat as it cooks. This section is cut into either petite chops or left as a whole rack of seven or eight ribs. Frenched racks have the bones scraped clean for a pretty restaurant-style finish. Two racks curved, bone side out, and tied into a circle form a crown roast. When stuffed and presented whole, it makes a spectacular entrée.

LOIN CUTS

➠ double loin chop
  loin chop
  loin roast
  tenderloin
  top loin chop

The loin is usually cut into loin chops or separated into top loin chops and the small tenderloin. When the entire loin section is left whole (bone-in), it is called a loin roast. A double loin roast with backbone intact is called a saddle. Rib and loin cuts are best cooked by dry heat (grilling, broiling, roasting or pan-frying). The lean, ultratender tenderloin is too small to roast without overcooking, so it's best suited to quick cooking methods, such as grilling, pan-frying or stir-frying.

ECONOMICAL CUTS

SHOULDER CUTS

➠ neck
  shoulder chop
  shoulder roast (bone-in or boneless)
  stewing cubes

Shoulder cuts are tougher and more flavourful than other cuts. They are tender enough to dry-roast but are even better braised, due to their ample fat content. Even shoulder chops are less chewy when quickly braised on the stove top rather than grilled.

FORESHANK CUTS

➠ foreshank
  rolled roast
  riblets
  spareribs

Both the hind shank and foreshank are excellent for braising and have rustic appeal. Shank is sometimes sliced into small lamb "osso buco" pieces.

BREAST CUTS

➠ ground breast
  sausage

The neck and breast yield small amounts; neck meat makes flavourful stocks, soups and stews, while breast meat is commonly ground for burgers and sausages.

VERSATILE CUTS

LEG CUTS

➠ whole leg (bone-in)
  short cut leg (bone-in)
  centre leg roast (bone-in)
  leg steak (bone-in)
  leg chop (bone-in)
  shank (bone-in)
  butterflied leg roast (boneless)
  sirloin roast (boneless)

In butchering, only hind legs are called lamb leg (front legs are called foreshanks). Leg is sold either whole or cut into small top (short cut, centre cut and leg steaks) and bottom (shank) portions. Though grilled short cut leg of lamb makes an impressive summer entrée, many people like the ease of carving a boneless roast, particularly one that has been butterflied to lie flat and cook quickly on the grill. Boneless leg meat is also the best choice for tender, flavourful kabobs. Leg cuts should be cooked using dry heat, such as grilling or roasting; steaks can also be pan-fried.

DONENESS TEMPERATURES

Expensive lamb rib and loin cuts should be cooked to no more than medium-rare (145°F/63°C). Economical and other cuts are also most flavourful and juicy when cooked to medium-rare, but they can be cooked more to taste. For medium, cook until an instant-read thermometer inserted in the thickest part reads 160°F (71°C); for well-done, it should read 170°F (77°C). Ground lamb should always be cooked to 160°F (71°C), just like all other ground red meats.

GROUND MEAT

RECIPES

BEEF & MUSHROOM CHEESEBURGERS

Rich, earthy cremini mushrooms and melty cheese glam up these hearty burgers. Chopping the mushrooms and incorporating them into the patties helps keep the extra-lean ground beef juicy.

8 **cremini mushrooms**

1 small **onion,** coarsely chopped

1 lb (450 g) **extra-lean ground beef**

1 tsp chopped **fresh thyme**

1 tsp **dry mustard**

½ tsp **salt**

¼ tsp each **black pepper** and **cayenne pepper**

4 slices **Cheddar cheese**

2 cups **baby arugula**

2 **tomatoes,** sliced

4 **whole grain kaiser rolls,** halved and toasted

In food processor, finely chop mushrooms with onion; scrape into large bowl.

Add beef, thyme, mustard, salt, black pepper and cayenne pepper; mix until combined. Shape into four ½-inch (1 cm) thick patties.

Grill, covered, on greased grill over medium-high heat, turning once, until no longer pink inside or instant-read thermometer inserted sideways in patties reads 160°F (71°C), 10 to 12 minutes.

Top each patty with Cheddar cheese. Sandwich with arugula and tomatoes in rolls.

Makes 4 burgers. PER BURGER: about 451 cal, 36 g pro, 18 g total fat (8 g sat. fat), 39 g carb, 7 g fibre, 82 mg chol, 780 mg sodium, 914 mg potassium. % RDI: 25% calcium, 33% iron, 18% vit A, 22% vit C, 30% folate.

FETA & LAMB BURGER PITAS

Ground lamb and feta cheese make this the ultimate Greek-style burger. Add leaf lettuce, sliced cucumbers and chopped tomatoes to the pitas for extra crunch and freshness.

¼ cup **plain yogurt**

1 tbsp chopped **fresh mint**

4 **pitas** (with pockets)

½ cup crumbled **feta cheese**

2 tbsp sliced **Kalamata olives**

PATTIES:

1 **egg**

¼ cup **dried bread crumbs**

Half **onion,** grated

2 cloves **garlic,** minced

2 tbsp **wine vinegar**

2 tsp **Dijon mustard**

½ tsp **dried oregano**

¼ tsp each **salt** and **pepper**

1 lb (450 g) **ground lamb**

PATTIES: In bowl, beat egg with 1 tbsp water; stir in bread crumbs, onion, garlic, vinegar, mustard, oregano, salt and pepper. Mix in lamb. Shape into four ¾-inch (2 cm) thick patties.

Grill, covered, on greased grill over medium heat, turning once, until no longer pink inside or instant-read thermometer inserted sideways in patties reads 160°F (71°C), 12 to 14 minutes.

Meanwhile, stir yogurt with mint.

Cut off top third of each pita; invert and place in bottom of pita. Place 1 patty in each; top patty with yogurt mixture. Sprinkle with feta cheese and olives.

Makes 4 pitas. PER PITA: about 478 cal, 33 g pro, 19 g total fat (9 g sat. fat), 43 g carb, 2 g fibre, 124 mg chol, 1,002 mg sodium, 482 mg potassium. % RDI: 20% calcium, 29% iron, 6% vit A, 2% vit C, 53% folate.

CHICKPEA SALAD WITH LEMON YOGURT DRESSING

The seasonings in this ultrafast salad make it a terrific side for Middle Eastern and Mediterranean cuisine alike. Try it with Feta & Lamb Burger Pitas (opposite) or any other burger.

In large bowl, stir together yogurt, lemon juice, salt and pepper.

Stir in chickpeas, tomatoes, celery, red onion, mint and parsley until well combined.

¼ cup **Balkan-style plain yogurt**

2 tbsp **lemon juice**

Pinch each **salt** and **pepper**

1 can (19 oz/540 mL) **chickpeas,** drained and rinsed

½ cup halved **grape tomatoes**

¼ cup diced **celery**

3 tbsp diced **red onion**

3 tbsp chopped **fresh mint**

2 tbsp chopped **fresh flat-leaf parsley**

TIP Fresh herbs add a ton of flavour to recipes, and keeping them fresh is the key to maintaining their appeal. When you bring them home, remove herbs from the packaging and wash well in a sinkful of cold water. Swish the leaves and let the grit settle. Lift them out of the water and pat dry with towels. Then wrap herbs in fresh towels, enclose in a plastic bag and store in the crisper drawer of the refrigerator. Use them lavishly and discard the leftovers when they wilt or the edges turn brown.

Makes 4 servings. PER SERVING: about 157 cal, 7 g pro, 2 g total fat (1 g sat. fat), 29 g carb, 6 g fibre, 3 mg chol, 307 mg sodium, 294 mg potassium. % RDI: 6% calcium, 14% iron, 5% vit A, 22% vit C, 36% folate.

PORK KOFTA PITAS WITH TOMATO SALSA

Turn a bountiful harvest of garden or farmer's market tomatoes into this tangy herbed salsa. It makes a wonderful topping for these savoury sandwiches or a nice change of pace from supermarket salsa with chips.

TOMATO SALSA: Combine tomatoes, green onion, dill, lemon juice, oil, salt and sugar; let stand for 10 minutes.

In large bowl, mix together pork, green onions, garlic, dill, paprika, coriander, salt, cumin, egg and 1 tbsp water. Divide into 8 portions; form each into egg shape. Thread onto metal or soaked wooden skewers.

Grill, covered, on greased grill over medium heat, turning once, until no longer pink inside, about 10 minutes.

Remove from skewers. Stuff 1 kofta into each pita half; surround with cucumber, onion and salsa.

1 lb (450 g) **lean ground pork**

2 **green onions,** minced

2 cloves **garlic,** minced

2 tbsp minced **fresh dill**

1½ tsp each **sweet paprika** and **ground coriander**

¾ tsp each **salt** and **ground cumin**

1 **egg,** beaten

4 **pitas,** halved

1 cup sliced **English cucumber**

Half small **red onion,** thinly sliced

TOMATO SALSA:

1 cup chopped seeded **tomatoes** (about 3)

1 **green onion,** thinly sliced

1 tbsp minced **fresh dill**

1 tbsp each **lemon juice** and **extra-virgin olive oil**

Pinch each **salt** and **granulated sugar**

Makes 4 pitas. PER PITA: about 433 cal, 29 g pro, 17 g total fat (5 g sat. fat), 40 g carb, 3 g fibre, 119 mg chol, 833 mg sodium, 620 mg potassium. % RDI: 10% calcium, 27% iron, 11% vit A, 20% vit C, 44% folate.

BLUE CHEESE-STUFFED BACON BURGERS

Chopped bacon in the meat mixture makes a burger that's smoky, extra juicy and utterly addictive. Add the ooey-gooey molten cheese centre and you have a burger fit for royalty.

4 slices **tomato**

4 **hamburger buns**

PATTIES:

1 **egg**

3 slices **bacon,** finely chopped

1 small **onion,** grated

2 tsp **Dijon mustard**

1 tsp **Worcestershire sauce**

½ tsp **dried thyme**

¼ tsp each **salt** and **pepper**

1 lb (450 g) **regular ground beef** or lean ground beef

½ cup crumbled **blue cheese**

PATTIES: In large bowl, beat egg; stir in bacon, onion, Dijon mustard, Worcestershire sauce, thyme, salt and pepper. Mix in beef.

Shape into 4 balls. With finger, make well in centre of each; stuff with one-quarter of the blue cheese. Press meat over to enclose cheese. Flatten into four ¾-inch (2 cm) thick patties.

Grill, covered, on greased grill over medium heat, turning once, until no longer pink inside or instant-read thermometer inserted sideways in patties reads 160°F (71°C), 12 to 14 minutes.

Sandwich patties and tomato in buns.

Makes 4 burgers. PER BURGER: about 528 cal, 31 g pro, 29 g total fat (13 g sat. fat), 34 g carb, 2 g fibre, 123 mg chol, 938 mg sodium, 475 mg potassium. % RDI: 19% calcium, 31% iron, 7% vit A, 5% vit C, 37% folate.

CHEDDAR MAPLE MUSTARD PORK BURGERS

Skewering the onion keeps the slices intact while grilling so they don't fall through the grates. Pork burgers need a little dressing up, and the sweet-spicy combo of mustard and maple really does the trick here.

PATTIES: In bowl, beat egg with 1 tbsp water; stir in Cheddar cheese, bread crumbs, garlic, salt, sage and pepper. Mix in pork. Shape into four ¾-inch (2 cm) thick patties.

Whisk together mustard, maple syrup and vinegar.

Cut onion into 4 generous ¼-inch (5 mm) thick slices. Push metal or soaked wooden skewer horizontally through centre of each slice.

Brush both sides of onion slices with oil; sprinkle with salt and pepper. Grill, covered, on greased grill over medium heat, turning once, until tender, about 10 minutes. Remove skewers.

Meanwhile, grill patties, covered, on greased grill over medium heat for 5 minutes.

Turn patties and brush with half of the mustard mixture; grill for 5 minutes.

Turn patties again and brush with remaining mustard mixture; grill until no longer pink inside or instant-read thermometer inserted sideways in patties reads 160°F (71°C), 2 to 4 minutes.

Sandwich patties and grilled onion in buns.

2 tbsp **Dijon mustard**
2 tbsp **maple syrup**
1 tsp **cider vinegar**
1 small **red onion**
1 tbsp **vegetable oil**
Pinch each **salt** and **pepper**
4 **hamburger buns**

PATTIES:
1 **egg**
¾ cup shredded **extra-old Cheddar cheese**
¼ cup **dried bread crumbs**
1 clove **garlic,** minced
½ tsp **salt**
½ tsp **dried sage**
¼ tsp **pepper**
1 lb (450 g) **lean ground pork**

Makes 4 burgers. PER BURGER: about 586 cal, 34 g pro, 28 g total fat (10 g sat. fat), 47 g carb, 3 g fibre, 140 mg chol, 979 mg sodium, 536 mg potassium. % RDI: 27% calcium, 28% iron, 8% vit A, 2% vit C, 39% folate.

MEATBALL STROGANOFF

**Meatballs offer a fun twist to this classic Russian-style main dish.
Serve with crusty bread or over egg noodles to soak up the creamy sauce.**

1 lb (450 g) **lean ground beef**

¼ cup **fresh bread crumbs**

1 **egg**

2 tsp **Worcestershire sauce**

1 clove **garlic,** minced

½ tsp each **salt** and **pepper**

1 tbsp **vegetable oil**

1 **onion,** chopped

3 cups sliced **mushrooms** (about 8 oz/225 g)

1 tsp **dried thyme**

½ cup **sodium-reduced beef broth**

1 tbsp **Dijon mustard**

⅓ cup **light sour cream**

2 tsp **cornstarch**

Mix together beef, bread crumbs, ¼ cup water, egg, Worcestershire sauce, garlic, salt and pepper. Roll by rounded 1 tbsp into balls. Bake on foil-lined rimmed baking sheet in 375°F (190°C) oven until instant-read thermometer inserted in centre of several reads 160°F (71°C), about 12 minutes.

Meanwhile, in large skillet, heat oil over medium heat; fry onion, mushrooms and thyme, stirring occasionally, until tender and no liquid remains, about 8 minutes.

Stir in broth and mustard; bring to boil. Reduce heat and simmer for 5 minutes.

Whisk together sour cream, 1 tbsp water and cornstarch; whisk into sauce. Add meatballs to skillet; simmer until sauce is thickened, about 2 minutes.

Makes 4 servings. PER SERVING: about 379 cal, 27 g pro, 22 g total fat (8 g sat. fat), 11 g carb, 2 g fibre, 118 mg chol, 566 mg sodium. % RDI: 8% calcium, 26% iron, 3% vit A, 3% vit C, 12% folate.

SMASHED POTATO SALAD

Sure, classic potato salad is always a hit at a barbecue, but this one is a delicious update
that guests will fall in love with. Smashing the potatoes results in a smoother, creamier salad,
and the gherkins give it a nice sweet-tart zing.

3 **eggs**

4 large **potatoes** (about 1½ lb/
    675 g total), peeled

Half **Vidalia onion** or sweet onion,
    finely chopped

2 ribs **celery,** diced

½ cup diced **sweet gherkin pickles**

½ cup **mayonnaise**

2 tbsp **Dijon mustard**

1 tbsp **cider vinegar**

¾ tsp **salt**

½ tsp **pepper**

¼ tsp **sweet paprika**

In saucepan, cover eggs with at least
1 inch (2.5 cm) cold water; cover and
bring to boil over high heat. Remove
from heat; let stand for 20 minutes.

Meanwhile, in large pot of boiling
salted water, cook potatoes until
fork-tender, about 15 minutes.
Drain and cut into chunks. Place in
large bowl.

Peel and chop eggs. Add to potatoes
along with onion, celery and sweet
gherkins, breaking up slightly with
potato masher.

Whisk together mayonnaise, mustard,
vinegar, salt, pepper and paprika; add
to potatoes. Mix well. Refrigerate until
chilled, about 1 hour.

Waxy potatoes – such as red-skinned, white and fingerling – are the best
choice for boiling and serving in salads. They have the perfect texture for
smashing in this chunky-smooth potato salad. They'll break up but not
disintegrate completely when you mash them.

Makes 8 servings. PER SERVING: about 208 cal, 4 g pro, 13 g total fat (2 g sat. fat), 20 g carb,
2 g fibre, 75 mg chol, 634 mg sodium, 315 mg potassium. % RDI: 3% calcium, 6% iron, 5% vit A,
12% vit C, 11% folate.

VEAL PATTY MELTS

Patty melts, an old-fashioned diner favourite, get a sophisticated flavour update with veal. Its delicate taste makes it worth the higher price tag.

In large skillet, heat oil over medium heat; cook onions, salt and pepper, stirring occasionally, until golden, about 10 minutes.

PATTIES: Meanwhile, in large bowl, whisk egg with 1 tbsp water; stir in garlic, parsley, mustard, salt, caraway seeds and pepper. Mix in veal. Shape into four ¾-inch (2 cm) thick patties.

Grill patties, covered, on greased grill over medium heat, turning once, until instant-read thermometer inserted sideways in patties reads 160°F (71°C), 12 to 14 minutes.

Spread mustard over 4 of the bread slices. Top with patties, Swiss cheese and fried onions; sandwich with remaining bread slices.

Grill sandwiches, covered, on greased grill over medium-low heat, turning once, until golden and cheese is melted, about 6 minutes. Cut in half.

2 tbsp **vegetable oil**
2 **onions,** sliced
Pinch each **salt** and **pepper**
2 tsp **Russian mustard** or sweet mustard
8 slices **dark rye bread**
4 oz (115 g) **Swiss cheese,** thinly sliced

PATTIES:
1 **egg**
1 clove **garlic,** minced
¼ cup chopped **fresh parsley**
1 tbsp **Dijon mustard**
½ tsp **salt**
¼ tsp **caraway seeds**
¼ tsp **pepper**
1 lb (450 g) **ground veal**

Makes 4 sandwiches. PER SANDWICH: about 513 cal, 38 g pro, 26 g total fat (9 g sat. fat), 31 g carb, 4 g fibre, 171 mg chol, 846 mg sodium, 535 mg potassium. % RDI: 33% calcium, 21% iron, 13% vit A, 12% vit C, 35% folate.

LAZY SHEPHERD'S PIE

No time to bake a shepherd's pie? This recipe turns that dish on its head by serving the savoury beef mixture over – instead of under – speedy mashed potatoes.

In large saucepan of boiling lightly salted water, cover and cook potatoes until tender, about 12 minutes. Drain and return to pot; shaking pan, dry over low heat, about 1 minute. Mash coarsely; stir in milk and green onion.

Meanwhile, in skillet, fry beef over medium-high heat, breaking up with spoon, until no longer pink, about 5 minutes. Using slotted spoon, transfer to plate.

Drain fat from pan; heat oil over medium heat. Fry mushrooms, onion, thyme, salt and pepper, stirring occasionally, until mushrooms are golden, about 8 minutes.

Whisk together broth, cornstarch and mustard; stir into pan. Add beef and peas; bring to boil. Reduce heat and simmer until thickened and heated through, about 5 minutes. Serve over mashed potatoes.

4 large **potatoes** (unpeeled), cubed (2 lb/900 g total)

¼ cup **milk** or buttermilk

1 **green onion,** sliced

1 lb (450 g) **lean ground beef**

1 tbsp **vegetable oil**

2½ cups small **mushrooms** (about 8 oz/225 g)

1 **onion,** diced

1 tsp **dried thyme**

¼ tsp each **salt** and **pepper**

1½ cups **sodium-reduced beef broth**

1 tbsp each **cornstarch** and **Dijon mustard**

1 cup **frozen peas**

Makes 4 servings. PER SERVING: about 488 cal, 30 g pro, 19 g total fat (7 g sat. fat), 50 g carb, 6 g fibre, 64 mg chol, 977 mg sodium, 1,267 mg potassium. % RDI: 7% calcium, 39% iron, 8% vit A, 50% vit C, 23% folate.

WAFU BURGERS

"Wafu" is a contraction of *washoku*, the Japanese word for "Japanese cooking." Serve this bunless burger (and its generous portions of grated radish and green onions) with rice and your favourite vegetables.

⅔ cup grated peeled **daikon radish** (about 6 oz/170 g)

2 **green onions,** minced

½ tsp grated **fresh ginger**

3 tbsp **ponzu** or sodium-reduced soy sauce

BURGERS:
1 **egg**

1 tbsp grated **fresh ginger**

1 tsp **sesame oil**

½ tsp **pepper**

¼ tsp **salt**

1 lb (450 g) **regular ground beef**

1 tbsp **vegetable oil**

Place daikon in cheesecloth-lined sieve; gently squeeze to remove some but not all of the liquid. Place in bowl; stir in green onions and ginger.

BURGERS: In large bowl, beat egg with 1 tbsp water; stir in ginger, sesame oil, pepper and salt. Mix in beef. Shape into four ¾-inch (2 cm) thick patties. *(Make-ahead: Layer between waxed paper in airtight container; refrigerate for up to 24 hours or freeze for up to 1 month.)*

In large skillet, heat vegetable oil over medium-high heat; cook patties, covered and turning once, until no longer pink inside or instant-read thermometer inserted sideways in patties reads 160°F (71°C), 10 to 12 minutes.

Serve topped with daikon mixture. Drizzle with ponzu.

Ponzu is a Japanese condiment that's making culinary inroads beyond its native country. You can find bottles of this sauce in Asian markets and even some supermarkets these days. A blend of citrus juice (traditionally from the sour Japanese yuzu fruit), soy sauce and vinegar, it gives a salty-sweet tang to recipes and is a delicious base for dipping sauces and dressings.

Makes 4 servings. PER SERVING: about 266 cal, 21 g pro, 18 g total fat (6 g sat. fat), 4 g carb, 1 g fibre, 99 mg chol, 673 mg sodium, 382 mg potassium. % RDI: 3% calcium, 19% iron, 3% vit A, 17% vit C, 14% folate.

CHINESE STEAMED BEEF PATTY

Weeknights require quick and easy dinners – but they shouldn't be boring. This tasty, meaty main has a touch of the exotic with all the convenience of a plain-old hamburger.

Soak mushrooms in hot water for 10 minutes. Drain and squeeze out water; chop. Using flat side of knife, crush water chestnuts.

In large bowl, combine mushrooms, water chestnuts, cornstarch, ginger, garlic, soy sauce, sesame oil, salt, pepper and all but 1 tbsp of the green onions; mix in beef.

Spread mixture in 9-inch (23 cm) pie plate to form large patty. Spread with hoisin sauce. Place rack or steamer in wok or large shallow pan; pour in enough water to come 1 inch (2.5 cm) below rack. Cover and bring to boil; reduce heat to medium-high.

Place pie plate on rack; cover and steam until no longer pink inside, about 15 minutes.

Remove pie plate from steamer; drain off fat. Sprinkle beef with remaining green onions. Serve with more hoisin sauce, if desired.

1 pkg (14 g) **dried shiitake mushrooms**

1 can (8 oz/227 mL) **water chestnuts,** drained and rinsed

1 tbsp **cornstarch**

2 tsp grated **fresh ginger**

1 clove **garlic,** minced

1 tsp each **soy sauce** and **sesame oil**

¼ tsp each **salt** and **pepper**

4 **green onions,** sliced

1 lb (450 g) **regular ground beef**

3 tbsp **hoisin sauce** (approx)

Makes 4 servings. PER SERVING: about 316 cal, 19 g pro, 20 g total fat (8 g sat. fat), 15 g carb, 2 g fibre, 64 mg chol, 480 mg sodium, 373 mg potassium. % RDI: 3% calcium, 19% iron, 1% vit A, 5% vit C, 10% folate.

CLASSIC CANADIAN TOURTIÈRE

Serve slices of this holiday staple with a generous helping of your favourite tomato-based chili sauce. The old-fashioned flaky pastry recipe is a great one to keep handy for all sorts of savoury pies.

1 large **potato** or 2 small potatoes, peeled and cubed

4 slices **thick-cut bacon,** chopped

1 **onion,** chopped

2 cloves **garlic,** minced

2 cups sliced **button mushrooms**

¼ cup **dry white wine**

1 lb (450 g) each **ground pork** and **ground veal**

½ tsp **salt**

¼ tsp **pepper**

¼ tsp **cinnamon**

Pinch **ground cloves**

All-Purpose Savoury Pie Dough (page 36)

1 **egg yolk**

In saucepan of boiling salted water, cook potato until tender, about 10 minutes. Drain and return to saucepan; mash.

Meanwhile, in large saucepan, fry bacon over medium-high heat until softened. Add onion and garlic; cook until softened, about 3 minutes.

Add mushrooms; cook until almost no liquid remains, 5 minutes. Add wine; cook until almost no liquid remains.

Stir in pork and veal; cook, breaking up with spoon, until browned, 20 to 25 minutes.

Add salt, pepper, cinnamon and cloves; cook, stirring, for 3 minutes. Add potato; cook, stirring, until incorporated, about 5 minutes. Let cool.

On floured surface, roll out 1 disc of the dough into 13-inch (33 cm) circle. Fit into 9-inch (23 cm) pie plate. Fill with meat mixture. Trim dough even with rim; brush edge with water.

Roll out remaining dough into 12-inch (30 cm) circle; arrange over filling, trimming to leave ½-inch (1 cm) overhang. Tuck under edge of bottom pastry; flute. Cut steam vents in top.

Roll out pastry scraps and cut out decorative shapes, if desired. Whisk egg yolk with 1 tbsp water; brush over pastry. Press shapes onto pastry; brush with egg wash.

Bake on bottom rack in 425°F (220°C) oven for 20 minutes. Reduce heat to 400°F (200°C); bake, covering edge with strips of foil if browning too quickly, until pastry is golden, about 30 minutes. Let stand for 10 minutes before cutting.

Makes 8 servings. PER SERVING: about 643 cal, 28 g pro, 41 g total fat (20 g sat. fat), 37 g carb, 2 g fibre, 159 mg chol, 594 mg sodium, 630 mg potassium. % RDI: 3% calcium, 23% iron, 13% vit A, 7% vit C, 41% folate.

ALL-PURPOSE SAVOURY PIE DOUGH

This recipe makes the perfect pie crust for Classic Canadian Tourtière (page 34), with enough extra pastry to cut decorative shapes from the scraps. For the holidays, try reindeer, snowflakes or stars for a pretty finish.

2½ cups **all-purpose flour**
¾ tsp **salt**
⅔ cup cold **unsalted butter,** cubed
⅓ cup cold **lard,** cubed
⅓ cup **cold water** (approx)

In bowl, whisk flour with salt. Using pastry blender or 2 knives, cut in butter and lard until in coarse crumbs with a few larger pieces.

Drizzle with water, tossing with fork until ragged dough forms and adding up to 1 tbsp more water if necessary.

Divide in half; shape into discs. Wrap each and refrigerate until chilled, about 30 minutes.

Makes enough for 1 double-crust 9-inch (23 cm) pie.

TURKISH FETA LAMB KABOBS

These juicy kabobs are so versatile. Serve them in warmed tomato sauce as a main dish alongside parsley-scented rice, or tuck them into pitas and top with mint-infused yogurt, cucumber and tomato for a classic Middle Eastern–style sandwich.

In large bowl, beat egg; stir in bread crumbs, mint, parsley, garlic, cumin, coriander, salt and pepper. Add lamb and feta cheese; mix just until combined. Shape into 16 balls; thread 4 onto each of 4 metal skewers. *(Make-ahead: Cover and refrigerate for up to 24 hours.)*

Grill, covered, on greased grill over medium heat, turning occasionally, until no longer pink in centre or instant-read thermometer inserted in several reads 160°F (71°C), about 12 minutes.

1 **egg**
¼ cup **fresh bread crumbs**
2 tbsp each chopped **fresh mint** and **fresh parsley**
4 cloves **garlic,** minced
1 tsp each **ground cumin** and **ground coriander**
¼ tsp each **salt** and **pepper**
1 lb (450 g) **lean ground lamb,** lean ground beef or a mixture of both
½ cup crumbled **feta cheese**

TIP If you're using soaked wooden skewers instead of metal ones, thread only 2 meatballs onto each for easier manoeuvring. Or omit the skewers and fry the meatballs in a bit of oil in a nonstick skillet over medium heat until no longer pink inside, about 10 minutes.

Makes 4 servings. PER SERVING: about 286 cal, 26 g pro, 18 g total fat (9 g sat. fat), 4 g carb, 1 g fibre, 144 mg chol, 435 mg sodium. % RDI: 12% calcium, 20% iron, 6% vit A, 5% vit C, 13% folate.

SPICY SAUSAGE CORN BREAD COBBLER

This mix of sausages, kale and potatoes is rustic, hearty and totally scrumptious underneath a crumbly corn bread topping. If you prefer a little less heat, substitute kielbasa or mild Italian sausages for the hot sausages.

In Dutch oven or large ovenproof saucepan, heat oil over medium-high heat; cook potatoes, stirring often, until beginning to brown, about 6 minutes.

Add onion and sausages; cook, stirring occasionally, until onion begins to soften, about 5 minutes.

Stir in broth, scraping up any browned bits; reduce heat, cover and simmer for 10 minutes. Stir in kale.

CORN BREAD TOPPING: Meanwhile, in bowl, whisk together flour, cornmeal, baking powder, baking soda and salt. Whisk together buttermilk, butter and egg; pour over flour mixture. Sprinkle with corn; stir just until combined. Spoon over sausage mixture.

Bake in 400°F (200°C) oven until topping is golden and no longer doughy underneath, 40 minutes. Let stand for 10 minutes before serving.

---

1 tbsp **olive oil**

3 cups cubed peeled **russet potatoes** (about 1½ large)

1 large **onion,** cut in ½-inch (1 cm) thick slices

1 lb (450 g) **hot Italian sausages,** sliced

2 cups **sodium-reduced beef broth**

4 cups chopped stemmed **kale**

CORN BREAD TOPPING:
1 cup **all-purpose flour**

½ cup **cornmeal**

2 tsp **baking powder**

½ tsp **baking soda**

½ tsp **salt**

1 cup **buttermilk**

2 tbsp **butter,** melted

1 **egg**

2 cups **frozen corn kernels,** thawed

Makes 6 to 8 servings. PER EACH OF 8 SERVINGS: about 416 cal, 17 g pro, 20 g total fat (7 g sat. fat), 44 g carb, 4 g fibre, 63 mg chol, 900 mg sodium, 720 mg potassium. % RDI: 14% calcium, 21% iron, 51% vit A, 75% vit C, 37% folate.

SPICED LAMB SAMOSAS

Spring roll wrappers are a quick and easy alternative to making fiddly samosa pastry. Dig your fine grater or rasp out of the drawer to grate the garlic and fresh ginger – it will yield the perfect texture. Serve these flavourful Indian treats with your favourite chutney (or try our favourite in the tip, below).

1 tbsp **vegetable oil**

1 small **sweet onion** (12 oz/340 g), diced

1 lb (450 g) **ground lamb**

2 cloves **garlic,** finely grated

1 tbsp finely grated **fresh ginger**

3 tbsp minced **green finger hot peppers** (seeded, if desired)

1¼ tsp **garam masala**

¾ tsp each **ground cumin** and **ground coriander**

¼ tsp each **ground allspice** and **cinnamon**

¾ tsp **salt**

⅓ cup **frozen peas**

¼ cup each chopped **fresh cilantro** and **green onion**

16 square (8-inch/20 cm) thawed **spring roll wrappers**

1 **egg yolk**

Vegetable oil for deep-frying

TIP To make our favourite Coriander Chutney, in food processor, purée together 4 cups fresh cilantro leaves; ¼ cup water; half green finger hot pepper, seeded; 4 tsp lemon juice; and ¼ tsp salt until smooth.

In large nonstick skillet, heat oil over medium-low heat; cook onion, stirring occasionally, until translucent, about 15 minutes. Transfer to plate.

In same skillet, sauté lamb over medium-high heat until no longer pink, about 5 minutes. Spoon off 2 tbsp of the fat and discard.

Add garlic, ginger and hot peppers; cook over medium heat, stirring often, for 3 minutes. Stir in garam masala, cumin, coriander, allspice, cinnamon and salt; cook for 3 minutes. Stir in peas and reserved onion. Stir in cilantro and green onion.

Cut spring roll sheets in half to make rectangles. Mix egg yolk with 1 tsp water; lightly brush over edges of pastry. Spoon 2 tbsp of the lamb filling about ½ inch (1 cm) from end of rectangle.

Fold 1 corner of wrapper over filling so bottom edge meets side edge to form triangle. Fold up triangle. Continue folding triangle sideways and upward to end. Fold flap over and adhere. Repeat with remaining wrappers and filling. *(Make-ahead: Freeze on baking sheets until firm. Transfer to airtight containers and freeze for up to 1 month. Cook from frozen.)*

In deep fryer or large deep saucepan, heat about 1½ inches (4 cm) oil until deep-fryer thermometer reads 350°F (180°C). Deep-fry samosas, in batches and turning once, until golden and heated through, about 4 minutes. Drain on paper towel–lined tray.

Makes 32 samosas. PER SAMOSA: about 79 cal, 3 g pro, 5 g total fat (2 g sat. fat), 5 g carb, trace fibre, 16 mg chol, 94 mg sodium, 56 mg potassium. % RDI: 1% calcium, 3% iron, 2% vit A, 5% vit C, 3% folate.

MOROCCAN-SPICED MEATBALLS IN SPICY TOMATO SAUCE

Need a little comfort when it's cold outside? These gently spiced meatballs simmering in fragrant tomato sauce are just the dish to warm you up.

In shallow Dutch oven, heat oil over medium-high heat; sauté onion until golden, about 6 minutes.

Add garlic, paprika, fennel seeds, cumin seeds, cayenne pepper, salt, and saffron (if using); cook, stirring, for 2 minutes. Stir in tomatoes, breaking up with spoon. Bring to boil; reduce heat and simmer until thickened slightly, about 1 hour.

MEATBALLS: Meanwhile, in large bowl, stir together onion, egg, bread crumbs, cilantro, olives, cumin seeds, oregano, salt, pepper and cinnamon; mix in beef. Roll by about 2 tbsp into 24 balls.

In large skillet, heat oil over medium-high heat; brown meatballs, in batches and turning often, 8 to 10 minutes. Drain on paper towel–lined plate. Add meatballs to sauce; simmer until meatballs are firm and sauce is thickened, about 20 minutes.

2 tbsp **vegetable oil**
1 **onion,** finely diced
3 cloves **garlic,** minced
2 tsp **sweet paprika**
1 tsp each **fennel seeds** and **cumin seeds,** crushed
½ tsp **cayenne pepper**
½ tsp **salt**
Pinch **saffron threads** (optional)
1 can (28 oz/796 mL) **whole tomatoes**

MEATBALLS:
1 small **onion,** grated
1 **egg**
⅓ cup **dried bread crumbs**
⅓ cup chopped **fresh cilantro**
¼ cup finely chopped **green olives**
1 tsp **cumin seeds,** crushed
1 tsp **dried oregano**
½ tsp each **salt** and **pepper**
¼ tsp **cinnamon**
1½ lb (675 g) **medium ground beef** or lean ground beef
2 tbsp **vegetable oil**

Makes 4 to 6 servings. PER EACH OF 6 SERVINGS: about 376 cal, 25 g pro, 25 g total fat (7 g sat. fat), 15 g carb, 3 g fibre, 93 mg chol, 760 mg sodium, 650 mg potassium. % RDI: 9% calcium, 34% iron, 8% vit A, 33% vit C, 15% folate.

MOUSSAKA-STYLE LAMB WITH ROASTED POTATOES

Moussaka is a layered dish held together with a rich béchamel sauce. This easy recipe has all the authentic flavours of the real thing but takes half the work and half the time – and contains fewer calories. Win, win, win!

1½ lb (675 g) **yellow-fleshed potatoes,** cut in ¼-inch (5 mm) thick slices

4 tsp **olive oil**

½ tsp each **salt** and **pepper**

1 **onion,** diced

3 cloves **garlic,** minced

1 small **eggplant,** diced

1½ tsp **dried oregano**

½ tsp **cinnamon**

1 lb (450 g) **ground lamb**

2 tbsp **tomato paste**

1 can (28 oz/796 mL) **diced tomatoes,** drained

½ cup **red wine**

¼ cup crumbled **feta cheese**

On parchment paper–lined baking sheet, toss together potatoes, half of the oil and pinch each of the salt and pepper. Bake on bottom rack in 400°F (200°C) oven, turning potatoes halfway through, until golden, about 30 minutes.

Meanwhile, in large Dutch oven, heat remaining oil over medium heat; cook onion and garlic, stirring occasionally, until slightly softened, 4 minutes.

Add eggplant, oregano, cinnamon and remaining salt and pepper; cook, stirring, until tender, about 6 minutes.

Crumble lamb into pan; cook, breaking up with spoon, until browned. Stir in tomato paste. Add tomatoes and wine; simmer until slightly thickened, about 10 minutes. Serve with roasted potatoes. Sprinkle with feta cheese.

Makes 4 servings. PER SERVING: about 512 cal, 27 g pro, 23 g total fat (10 g sat. fat), 48 g carb, 7 g fibre, 83 mg chol, 664 mg sodium, 1,580 mg potassium. % RDI: 14% calcium, 36% iron, 6% vit A, 58% vit C, 42% folate.

PORK PIE WITH OKA MASH

This twist on shepherd's pie features smoky, spicy chorizo and flavourful Oka cheese (a Canadian must-try if you haven't had it before). It's a superb all-in-one meal for a relaxed night in.

1 tbsp **olive oil**

2 **leeks,** trimmed and thinly sliced

3 cloves **garlic,** minced

2 lb (900 g) **lean ground pork**

4 oz (115 g) **dry-cured chorizo,** cubed

2 cups **sodium-reduced beef broth**

⅓ cup **all-purpose flour**

1 **sweet potato,** peeled and finely chopped

1 tsp **smoked paprika**

¼ tsp each **salt** and **pepper**

Pinch **cinnamon**

1 cup **frozen peas**

TOPPING:

3 lb (1.35 kg) **russet potatoes,** peeled and quartered

2 cloves **garlic**

1 cup **milk**

8 oz (225 g) **Oka cheese,** shredded

2 tbsp **butter**

In large saucepan, heat oil over medium heat; cook leeks and garlic, stirring occasionally, until softened, about 6 minutes. Transfer to bowl.

In same pan, brown pork and chorizo over medium-high heat, breaking up pork with spoon, about 5 minutes. Add ¼ cup of the broth; cook, scraping up browned bits, until no liquid remains. Stir in flour; cook, stirring, for 2 minutes.

Gradually stir in remaining broth; bring to boil. Stir in leek mixture, sweet potato, paprika, salt, pepper and cinnamon; return to boil. Reduce heat and simmer, stirring often, until slightly thickened, about 15 minutes. Stir in peas; scrape into 13- x 9-inch (3 L) baking dish.

TOPPING: Meanwhile, in large saucepan of boiling salted water, cook potatoes and garlic until tender, about 20 minutes. Drain and return to pan; mash with milk, Oka cheese and butter. Spread over pork mixture. *(Make-ahead: Let cool. Cover with plastic wrap and overwrap in heavy-duty foil; freeze for up to 2 months. Thaw in refrigerator for 24 hours; remove plastic wrap, re-cover with foil and bake in 400°F/200°C oven for 35 minutes. Increase heat to 425°F/ 220°C; bake, uncovered, until topping is golden, about 10 minutes.)*

Bake in 400°F (200°C) oven until filling is bubbly and topping is golden, about 25 minutes.

Makes 8 to 10 servings. PER EACH OF 10 SERVINGS: about 523 cal, 30 g pro, 29 g total fat (13 g sat. fat), 34 g carb, 3 g fibre, 105 mg chol, 549 mg sodium, 841 mg potassium. % RDI: 20% calcium, 17% iron, 47% vit A, 23% vit C, 19% folate.

CABBAGE ROLLS

This big-batch dish also freezes beautifully – wrap the cooled pan in plastic wrap, then foil, and freeze for up to 2 weeks. Thaw in the fridge for 48 hours, then reheat, covered, in 350°F (180°C) oven for about 1 hour. Braise any leftover cabbage for a quick weeknight side dish or shred it and add to salads or stir-fries.

Core cabbages. In large pot of boiling salted water, blanch cabbages, 1 at a time, until leaves are softened, 5 to 8 minutes. Chill under cold water. Working from core end, carefully pull 12 leaves off each, returning cabbages to boiling water for 2 to 3 minutes when leaves become difficult to remove. Drain leaves on tea towels; cut out coarse veins. Set leaves aside. Reserve remaining cabbage.

In Dutch oven, melt butter over medium-high heat; sauté onions, caraway seeds, salt and pepper until golden, 10 minutes. Add sugar; cook for 2 minutes. Add tomatoes; bring to boil. Reduce heat and simmer until thickened, 30 minutes. Set aside.

FILLING: In saucepan, melt butter over medium heat; cook onions, garlic, thyme and cayenne pepper, stirring often, until softened, 10 minutes.

Add rice; cook, stirring, for 1 minute. Add broth; bring to boil. Reduce heat, cover and simmer until rice is tender and liquid is absorbed, 20 minutes. Transfer to large bowl; let cool for 5 minutes. Stir in pork, parsley, dill, egg, salt and pepper.

Spread 1 cup of the tomato mixture in 24-cup (6 L) roasting pan or Dutch oven. Spoon scant ¼ cup filling onto centre of each of the 24 reserved leaves; fold 1 end and sides over filling. Roll up. Arrange half of the rolls, seam side down, in pan; top with half of the remaining tomato mixture. Arrange remaining rolls on top; top with remaining tomato mixture, then enough of the remaining cabbage leaves to cover and prevent scorching.

Cover and bake in 350°F (180°C) oven until tender, about 2 hours. *(Make-ahead: Let cool. Refrigerate for up to 24 hours.)*

2 heads (each 2 lb/900 g) **Savoy cabbage** or green cabbage
2 tbsp **butter**
2 large **white onions,** sliced
¼ tsp **caraway seeds,** crushed
¼ tsp each **salt** and **pepper**
3 tbsp packed **brown sugar**
2 cans (each 28 oz/796 mL) **crushed tomatoes**

FILLING:
2 tbsp **butter**
3 **onions,** chopped
4 cloves **garlic,** minced
½ tsp **dried thyme**
Pinch **cayenne pepper**
½ cup **long-grain rice**
1¼ cups **sodium-reduced chicken broth**
1½ lb (675 g) **lean ground pork,** lean ground beef or a mixture of both
½ cup chopped **fresh parsley**
2 tbsp chopped **fresh dill** (or 1 tsp dried dillweed)
1 **egg,** beaten
¾ tsp each **salt** and **pepper**

Makes 8 servings. PER SERVING: about 411 cal, 22 g pro, 22 g total fat (9 g sat. fat), 33 g carb, 5 g fibre, 93 mg chol, 860 mg sodium. % RDI: 10% calcium, 22% iron, 21% vit A, 65% vit C, 21% folate.

CLASSIC LASAGNA

Lasagna is the go-to meal for a crowd, and everyone always asks for seconds. Packed with noodles, simple meaty tomato sauce and plenty of creamy cheese, this recipe is the gold standard for lasagnas.

TOMATO MEAT SAUCE: In Dutch oven, heat oil over medium heat; cook onions, celery, carrot and garlic, stirring occasionally, until softened, about 5 minutes.

Add beef; cook, breaking up with spoon, until browned and no liquid remains, about 6 minutes.

Stir in tomato paste. Add tomatoes, wine, bay leaves, oregano and pepper; simmer, stirring occasionally, until slightly thickened, about 40 minutes. Stir in basil. Discard bay leaves. *(Make-ahead: Let cool for 30 minutes. Refrigerate in airtight container for up to 3 days.)*

Meanwhile, in pot of boiling salted water, cook noodles for 2 minutes less than package directions for al dente. Drain and arrange noodles in single layer on tea towels.

Stir together ricotta cheese, eggs and pepper. In 13- x 9-inch (3 L) baking dish, spread 1½ cups of the meat sauce. Arrange 3 noodles over top; sprinkle with half of the mozzarella cheese. Top with 2½ cups of the meat sauce, 3 noodles, ricotta mixture, 3 noodles, 2½ cups of the meat sauce, 3 noodles, then remaining meat sauce and mozzarella cheese. Sprinkle with Parmesan cheese. *(Make-ahead: Cover with plastic wrap and refrigerate for up to 3 days; remove plastic wrap.)*

Cover with foil. Bake in 375°F (190°C) oven for 45 minutes. Uncover and bake until cheese is golden, about 15 minutes. Loosely cover with foil; let stand for 30 minutes before serving.

12 **lasagna noodles**
1 tub (475 g) **extra-smooth ricotta cheese**
2 **eggs**
Pinch **pepper**
3 cups shredded **mozzarella cheese**
1 cup grated **Parmesan cheese**

TOMATO MEAT SAUCE:
2 tbsp **olive oil**
2 **onions,** diced
1 rib **celery,** diced
1 **carrot,** diced
4 cloves **garlic,** minced
1½ lb (675 g) **lean ground beef**
⅓ cup **tomato paste**
2 cans (each 28 oz/796 mL) **diced tomatoes**
1 cup **red wine** or white wine
2 **bay leaves**
1 tsp **dried oregano**
½ tsp **pepper**
2 tbsp chopped **fresh basil**

Makes 12 servings. PER SERVING: about 474 cal, 31 g pro, 25 g total fat (12 g sat. fat), 31 g carb, 3 g fibre, 113 mg chol, 585 mg sodium, 669 mg potassium. % RDI: 38% calcium, 25% iron, 26% vit A, 35% vit C, 15% folate.

OVEN-ROASTED GRAPE TOMATOES

This zippy side dish makes a great foil for rich Orange Fennel Sausage Patties (opposite).
It's easy to assemble and pop into the oven while you're frying the patties.

4 cups **grape tomatoes** or halved cherry tomatoes

2 tbsp **extra-virgin olive oil**

2 cloves **garlic,** sliced

½ tsp **dried oregano**

¼ tsp **salt**

Pinch **hot pepper flakes** (optional)

In 13- x 9-inch (3 L) baking dish, toss together tomatoes, oil, garlic, oregano, salt, and hot pepper flakes (if using).

Roast in 400°F (200°C) oven, stirring occasionally, until shrivelled, about 25 minutes.

Fresh tomatoes – whether they're beefsteak, plum, grape or cherry – always taste better when they're stored at room temperature. Refrigerating tomatoes makes their flesh mealy and unpleasant, whether cooked or served fresh. Store tomatoes on the counter, out of direct sunlight, for a few days. Toss any that are wrinkled or develop dark spots.

Makes 8 servings. PER SERVING: about 45 cal, 1 g pro, 4 g total fat (1 g sat. fat), 3 g carb, 1 g fibre, 0 mg chol, 76 mg sodium, 181 mg potassium. % RDI: 1% calcium, 2% iron, 6% vit A, 15% vit C, 4% folate.

ORANGE FENNEL SAUSAGE PATTIES

**These homemade sausages taste best when assembled ahead
so the flavours have a chance to develop. It may seem a little strange,
but making a depression in the top of each patty helps it cook to an even thickness.**

Using spice grinder or mortar and pestle, crush fennel seeds.

In large bowl, mix together pork, bacon, garlic, ⅓ cup water, orange zest, salt, savory, hot pepper flakes, pepper and fennel seeds just until combined.

Form by scant ¼ cups into sixteen ½-inch (1 cm) thick patties. Cover and refrigerate for 1 hour. *(Make-ahead: Refrigerate for up to 12 hours. Or layer between waxed paper in airtight container and freeze for up to 2 weeks. Thaw in refrigerator.)*

With thumb and index finger, make depression in top of each patty.

In nonstick skillet, fry patties, in batches and turning once, until browned and instant-read thermometer inserted sideways in patties reads 160°F (71°C), 10 to 12 minutes.

2 tsp **fennel seeds**

12 oz (340 g) **lean ground pork**

9 slices **bacon,** chopped

2 cloves **garlic,** minced

2 tsp grated **orange zest**

1 tsp **salt**

1 tsp **dried savory** or dried thyme

½ tsp **hot pepper flakes**

½ tsp **pepper**

Makes 8 servings. PER SERVING: about 115 cal, 11 g pro, 8 g total fat (3 g sat. fat), 1 g carb, trace fibre, 32 mg chol, 477 mg sodium, 173 mg potassium. % RDI: 2% calcium, 5% iron, 1% vit A, 2% vit C, 1% folate.

CHILI MAC

This crowd-pleaser is fun to eat thanks to the crazily shaped noodles – perfect for enticing kids to the table. Garnish each serving with shredded Cheddar cheese, green onions and sour cream, if desired.

1½ lb (675 g) **extra-lean ground beef**

1 tbsp **olive oil**

1 small **onion,** chopped

2 ribs **celery,** chopped

2 **carrots,** chopped

2 cloves **garlic,** minced

2 tbsp **chili powder**

1 tsp **ground cumin**

½ tsp **dried thyme**

¼ tsp **pepper**

1 can (28 oz/796 mL) **crushed tomatoes**

1 can (28 oz/796 mL) **diced tomatoes**

1 can (19 oz/540 mL) **kidney beans,** drained and rinsed

3 tbsp packed **brown sugar**

2 tbsp **Worcestershire sauce**

4 cups **radiatore pasta** or other short pasta

In Dutch oven or large saucepan, cook beef over medium-high heat, breaking up with spoon, until no longer pink. Drain in sieve.

Add oil to pan; sauté onion, celery, carrots, garlic, chili powder, cumin, thyme and pepper until carrots begin to soften, about 8 minutes.

Stir in crushed and diced tomatoes, beans, brown sugar, Worcestershire sauce and beef; reduce heat, cover and simmer until celery is tender, about 20 minutes.

Meanwhile, in large saucepan of boiling salted water, cook pasta according to package directions until al dente; drain and stir into chili.

Makes 8 to 10 servings. PER EACH OF 10 SERVINGS: about 355 cal, 23 g pro, 8 g total fat (3 g sat. fat), 49 g carb, 8 g fibre, 37 mg chol, 544 mg sodium, 863 mg potassium. % RDI: 9% calcium, 41% iron, 37% vit A, 35% vit C, 49% folate.

GROUND BEEF CHILI

Whether it's for Super Bowl Sunday or any other day, this chili is a hearty classic. For those who can take the heat, include the optional cayenne pepper (and up it a notch or two for a five-alarm version).

1 tbsp **vegetable oil**

3 **onions,** chopped

4 cloves **garlic,** minced

2 lb (900 g) **medium ground beef**
  or lean ground beef

3 tbsp **chili powder**

1¼ tsp **ground cumin**

1 tsp **ground coriander**

1 tsp **dried oregano**

1 tsp **salt**

¼ tsp **pepper**

¼ tsp **cayenne pepper** (optional)

1 can (28 oz/796 mL) **plum tomatoes**

½ cup **bottled strained tomatoes**
  (passata)

1 can (19 oz/540 mL) **kidney beans,**
  drained and rinsed

In Dutch oven or large saucepan, heat oil over medium heat; cook onions and garlic, stirring occasionally, until golden, 8 to 10 minutes.

Add beef; cook, breaking up with spoon, until no longer pink. Stir in chili powder, cumin, coriander, oregano, salt, pepper, and cayenne pepper (if using); cook for 1 minute.

Crush plum tomatoes with potato masher; add to pan along with strained tomatoes, ½ cup water and beans. Bring to boil; reduce heat, cover and simmer for 20 minutes. Uncover and cook for 10 minutes.

Makes 6 to 8 servings. PER EACH OF 8 SERVINGS: about 373 cal, 26 g pro, 21 g total fat (8 g sat. fat), 20 g carb, 6 g fibre, 68 mg chol, 696 mg sodium, 747 mg potassium. % RDI: 8% calcium, 34% iron, 10% vit A, 28% vit C, 18% folate.

CINCINNATI CHILI

This beanless regional specialty is a point of pride in Cincinnati, where fierce loyalty divides the city over which restaurant serves the best version. Cooked low and slow, with the distinguishing flavours of cinnamon and cocoa, this meaty, saucy chili is served over spaghetti.

In large nonstick skillet, cook beef over medium heat, breaking up with spoon, until no longer pink, about 5 minutes. Drain off fat. *(Make-ahead: Cover and refrigerate for up to 24 hours.)*

In slow cooker, stir together beef, tomatoes, broth, tomato paste, onion, garlic, cocoa powder, oregano, cinnamon, salt and pepper.

Cover and cook on low until thick enough to mound on spoon and tomatoes are broken down, 7 to 8 hours.

Whisk flour with 1 tbsp water; stir into chili. Cover and cook on high until thickened, about 15 minutes.

In large pot of boiling salted water, cook pasta according to package directions until al dente; drain. Serve topped with chili; sprinkle with Cheddar cheese.

2 lb (900 g) **lean ground beef**

1 can (28 oz/796 mL) **whole tomatoes**

1 cup **sodium-reduced beef broth**

¼ cup **tomato paste**

1 **onion,** chopped

2 cloves **garlic,** minced

1 tbsp **cocoa powder**

2 tsp **dried oregano**

1 tsp **cinnamon**

¼ tsp each **salt** and **pepper**

1 tbsp **all-purpose flour**

12 oz (340 g) **spaghetti**

1 cup shredded **Cheddar cheese**

Makes 6 to 8 servings. PER EACH OF 8 SERVINGS: about 489 cal, 33 g pro, 21 g total fat (9 g sat. fat), 41 g carb, 4 g fibre, 83 mg chol, 556 mg sodium, 677 mg potassium. % RDI: 16% calcium, 39% iron, 6% vit A, 27% vit C, 49% folate.

LASAGNA PASTA TOSS

Enjoy the comforting taste of lasagna in less than half the time it usually takes to make. If you can't find pappardelle pasta, substitute an equal weight of fresh lasagna sheets and cut each lengthwise into eight strips.

RICOTTA HERB TOPPING: Stir together ricotta cheese, parsley, lemon zest, lemon juice and nutmeg.

In saucepan, heat oil over medium-high heat; cook onion, stirring occasionally, until softened, about 4 minutes.

Stir in beef, garlic, Italian herb seasoning, salt and pepper; cook, breaking up beef with spoon, until no longer pink, about 6 minutes.

Stir in mushrooms; cook until light golden, about 6 minutes. Stir in tomatoes and bring to boil; reduce heat and simmer for 15 minutes.

Meanwhile, in large pot of boiling lightly salted water, cook pasta according to package directions until al dente. Drain and return to pot. Add beef mixture; toss to coat. Serve topped with dollops of ricotta cheese mixture.

1 tbsp **olive oil**

1 **onion,** finely diced

1 lb (450 g) **extra-lean ground beef**

3 cloves **garlic,** minced

2 tsp **dried Italian herb seasoning**

½ tsp each **salt** and **pepper**

6 oz (170 g) **button mushrooms,** stemmed and quartered

1 bottle (680 mL) **strained tomatoes** (passata)

12 oz (340 g) **pappardelle pasta**

RICOTTA HERB TOPPING:

⅔ cup **ricotta cheese**

2 tbsp chopped **fresh parsley**

½ tsp grated **lemon zest**

½ tsp **lemon juice**

Pinch grated **nutmeg**

Makes 4 servings. PER SERVING: about 686 cal, 43 g pro, 19 g total fat (8 g sat. fat), 83 g carb, 8 g fibre, 83 mg chol, 980 mg sodium, 1,116 mg potassium. % RDI: 18% calcium, 61% iron, 21% vit A, 47% vit C, 98% folate.

ROMAINE SALAD WITH LEMON VINAIGRETTE

This lemony salad is the perfect light-as-a-feather foil for filling dishes, such as Whole Grain Rotini With Lamb Ragout (opposite). Toss in a handful of croutons, sliced cucumbers or shaved fennel if you want a little extra crunch.

⅓ cup **olive oil**

3 tbsp **lemon juice**

2 tsp chopped **fresh dill**

1 tsp **Dijon mustard**

½ tsp **salt**

¼ tsp each **granulated sugar** and **pepper**

1 head **romaine lettuce**

½ cup shredded **radicchio**

½ cup thinly sliced **radishes**

Whisk together oil, lemon juice, dill, mustard, salt, sugar and pepper.

Tear romaine lettuce into bite-size pieces. In large bowl, toss together romaine, radicchio and radishes; add dressing. Toss to coat.

This salad features sturdy lettuces (romaine and radicchio) and radishes, which means it's great for making ahead for a party or potluck. Prep the salad mixture and cover it with a damp paper towel, then cover loosely with plastic wrap. Then make the vinaigrette and pour it into an airtight container (a canning jar makes a great take-and-shake receptacle). Store both in the fridge for up to 2 days. Toss together just before serving.

Makes 8 servings. PER SERVING: about 96 cal, 1 g pro, 9 g total fat (1 g sat. fat), 3 g carb, 1 g fibre, 0 mg chol, 160 mg sodium. % RDI: 3% calcium, 7% iron, 22% vit A, 37% vit C, 52% folate.

WHOLE GRAIN ROTINI WITH LAMB RAGOUT

Whole grain pasta is rustic enough to stand up well to a thick lamb-and-tomato sauce. Topping it with creamy ricotta and fresh mint adds a touch of elegance.

In large skillet, heat oil over medium heat; cook onion, garlic and Italian herb seasoning until fragrant, about 2 minutes. Add lamb; cook over medium-high heat, breaking up with spoon, until lightly browned, about 3 minutes. Drain off all but 1 tsp fat.

Add zucchini; cook for 2 minutes. Add tomatoes, salt and pepper; bring to boil. Reduce heat and simmer until sauce is thickened and zucchini is tender, about 10 minutes.

Meanwhile, in saucepan of boiling salted water, cook pasta according to package directions until al dente; drain. Add to sauce and toss to coat. Top each serving with ricotta cheese; sprinkle with mint.

2 tsp **olive oil**

1 small **onion,** chopped

2 cloves **garlic,** chopped

1 tsp **dried Italian herb seasoning**

1 lb (450 g) **ground lamb**

2 **zucchini,** cut in ½-inch (1 cm) cubes

1 bottle (680 mL) **strained tomatoes** (passata)

¼ tsp each **salt** and **pepper**

4 cups **whole grain rotini pasta**

½ cup **light ricotta cheese**

2 tbsp chopped **fresh mint**

Makes 4 servings. PER SERVING: about 519 cal, 32 g pro, 19 g total fat (8 g sat. fat), 52 g carb, 7 g fibre, 75 mg chol, 794 mg sodium, 914 mg potassium. % RDI: 14% calcium, 53% iron, 15% vit A, 13% vit C, 60% folate.

WHOLE GRAIN ROTINI WITH LAMB RAGOUT page 57

FRESH PASTA WITH LAMB & CURRANT MEATBALLS

Tomato-based spaghetti and meatballs may be everyone's favourite, but you really need to try this heavenly Middle Eastern take on that standard dish. Serve with green beans, asparagus or a simple salad – our Romaine Salad With Lemon Vinaigrette (page 56) is an excellent choice.

1¼ cups **sodium-reduced chicken broth**

¼ cup chopped **fresh parsley**

1 tbsp **all-purpose flour**

1 tbsp **lemon juice**

1 tsp chopped **fresh rosemary**

½ tsp chopped **fresh thyme**

1 pkg (350 g) **fresh linguine pasta**

MEATBALLS:

1 lb (450 g) **ground lamb** or lean ground beef

½ cup **dried bread crumbs**

¼ cup **dried currants**

1 tbsp **Dijon mustard**

½ tsp grated **lemon zest**

½ tsp **salt**

¼ tsp **pepper**

1 **egg**

2 tsp **olive oil**

1 **onion,** diced

2 cloves **garlic,** minced

MEATBALLS: In bowl, combine lamb, bread crumbs, currants, mustard, lemon zest, salt, pepper and egg; set aside.

In large nonstick skillet, heat oil over medium heat; cook onion and garlic, stirring frequently, until onion begins to soften, about 5 minutes. Scrape half into small bowl; set aside. Stir remaining onion mixture into lamb mixture until combined. Shape into 20 balls.

In same skillet, cook meatballs over medium-high heat, turning often, until browned, about 8 minutes. Drain off fat; add reserved onion mixture.

Whisk together broth, parsley, flour, lemon juice, rosemary and thyme; add to pan and bring to simmer. Cook, stirring occasionally, until thickened and instant-read thermometer inserted in several meatballs reads 160°F (71°C), about 3 minutes.

Meanwhile, in large pot of boiling lightly salted water, cook pasta according to package directions until al dente.

Reserving ¼ cup of the cooking liquid, drain pasta and return to pot. Add meatball mixture. Toss to coat, adding as much of the reserved cooking liquid as needed to coat pasta.

Makes 4 servings. PER SERVING: about 632 cal, 35 g pro, 23 g total fat (9 g sat. fat), 70 g carb, 4 g fibre, 183 mg chol, 919 mg sodium, 559 mg potassium. % RDI: 8% calcium, 36% iron, 7% vit A, 12% vit C, 83% folate.

SLOW COOKER SPAGHETTI & MEATBALLS

This is a terrific Saturday night meal. Set up the slow cooker in the morning, then pop out and do all your errands. When you get home, toss together a green salad while the spaghetti is boiling for a low-fuss meal. Dinner is done!

1 tbsp **extra-virgin olive oil**

1 **onion,** chopped

2 cloves **garlic,** minced

½ tsp each **dried oregano** and **hot pepper flakes**

1 can (28 oz/796 mL) **crushed tomatoes**

¼ cup minced **fresh parsley**

1 lb (450 g) **spaghetti,** cooked

MEATBALLS:

1 **egg**

½ cup grated **onion**

1 large clove **garlic,** minced

¼ cup **dried bread crumbs**

¼ cup grated **Parmesan cheese**

½ tsp each **dried basil, dried oregano** and **pepper**

¼ tsp **salt**

1 lb (450 g) **lean ground beef**

MEATBALLS: In large bowl, beat egg; stir in onion, garlic, bread crumbs, Parmesan cheese, basil, oregano, pepper and salt. Mix in beef. Shape into 16 balls. Bake on foil-lined rimmed baking sheet in 400°F (200°C) oven until firm, about 10 minutes. Transfer to slow cooker.

Meanwhile, in skillet, heat oil over medium heat; cook onion, garlic, oregano and hot pepper flakes, stirring occasionally, until onion is softened, about 5 minutes. Add to slow cooker.

Stir in tomatoes; cover and cook on low until slightly thickened, 4 to 6 hours. Stir in minced parsley; serve with spaghetti.

Makes 4 servings. PER SERVING: about 848 cal, 46 g pro, 25 g total fat (9 g sat. fat), 111 g carb, 11 g fibre, 119 mg chol, 738 mg sodium, 1,152 mg potassium. % RDI: 20% calcium, 72% iron, 21% vit A, 42% vit C, 128% folate.

SAUSAGE & SWISS CHARD RIGATONI

Even picky eaters will love the combination of sausage, pasta and mellow, sweet Swiss chard in this dish. It's easy to make on a weeknight but delicious enough for a laid-back dinner with friends.

In large skillet, heat oil over medium-high heat; sauté sausage meat, breaking up with spoon, until no longer pink, about 8 minutes. Stir in garlic and hot pepper flakes; cook for 2 minutes.

Add tomatoes, basil, salt and sugar; bring to boil. Reduce heat and simmer for 20 minutes. Stir in beans. *(Make-ahead: Let cool. Refrigerate in airtight container for up to 24 hours.)*

Meanwhile, in large saucepan of boiling salted water, cook pasta until still slightly firm in centre, about 8 minutes. Reserving ½ cup of the cooking liquid, drain pasta and return to pot. Add sauce, reserved cooking liquid and Swiss chard; toss to coat. Transfer to 10-cup (2.5 L) baking dish.

Sprinkle with mozzarella and Parmesan cheeses; cover with greased foil. Bake in 375°F (190°C) oven for 20 minutes. Uncover and bake until bubbly and browned, about 10 minutes.

4 tsp **olive oil**

3 **Italian sausages** (12 oz/340 g total), casings removed

3 cloves **garlic,** minced

½ tsp **hot pepper flakes**

1 can (28 oz/796 mL) **diced tomatoes**

¼ cup chopped **fresh basil**

¼ tsp **salt**

Pinch **granulated sugar**

1 cup rinsed drained **canned navy beans**

5 cups **mezzi rigatoni pasta** or rigatoni pasta (12 oz/340 g)

8 cups chopped **Swiss chard** (13 oz/380 g)

⅔ cup shredded **mozzarella cheese**

¼ cup grated **Parmesan cheese**

Makes 6 to 8 servings. PER EACH OF 8 SERVINGS: about 393 cal, 18 g pro, 16 g total fat (6 g sat. fat), 44 g carb, 4 g fibre, 34 mg chol, 871 mg sodium, 643 mg potassium. % RDI: 16% calcium, 32% iron, 18% vit A, 37% vit C, 50% folate.

SPICY PORK NOODLE STIR-FRY

This one-dish meal comes together quickly, so be sure to have all of the prep finished before you start cooking. If you don't like spice, omit the chili garlic paste or serve it as a condiment on the side.

In large bowl, soak vermicelli in warm water until softened and separated, about 5 minutes. Drain and set aside.

Meanwhile, whisk together soy sauce, chili garlic paste, vinegar, sugar, sesame oil, salt and 1⅔ cups water; set aside.

In wok or large skillet over medium-high heat, cook pork, stirring occasionally and breaking up with spoon, until no longer pink, about 5 minutes. With slotted spoon, transfer pork to bowl.

Drain fat from wok; wipe clean. Return to heat and add vegetable oil and mushrooms; cook, stirring often, until mushrooms begin to soften, about 2 minutes. Add coleslaw mix, snow peas, green onions and garlic; stir-fry for 2 minutes.

Stir in pork, soy sauce mixture and noodles, tossing to combine; stir-fry until tender, about 3 minutes. Sprinkle with peanuts.

8 oz (225 g) **rice stick vermicelli** (about ⅛ inch/3 mm wide)

¼ cup **sodium-reduced soy sauce**

4 tsp **chili garlic paste** (such as sambal oelek)

1 tbsp **seasoned rice vinegar**

2 tsp **granulated sugar**

2 tsp **sesame oil**

¼ tsp **salt**

1 lb (450 g) **lean ground pork**

2 tsp **vegetable oil**

2 cups sliced **shiitake mushrooms**

2 cups **coleslaw mix**

1 cup **snow peas,** trimmed and thinly sliced

4 **green onions,** thinly sliced

4 cloves **garlic,** minced

⅓ cup chopped **unsalted roasted peanuts**

Makes 4 servings. PER SERVING: about 588 cal, 30 g pro, 24 g total fat (6 g sat. fat), 63 g carb, 6 g fibre, 67 mg chol, 892 mg sodium, 617 mg potassium. % RDI: 7% calcium, 20% iron, 12% vit A, 28% vit C, 20% folate.

PENNE WITH SMOKED SAUSAGE & BROCCOLI

There are many varieties of smoked sausage, so choose your favourite for this hearty recipe. This is definitely a saltier dish, so ease up on your sodium intake the rest of the day to make room for it in your diet.

2 tbsp **extra-virgin olive oil**

12 oz (340 g) **smoked sausage,** sliced

2 **onions,** chopped

2 cloves **garlic,** minced

1 tsp **dried Italian herb seasoning**

½ tsp **pepper**

1 can (28 oz/796 mL) **whole tomatoes**

¼ cup **tomato paste**

¼ cup chopped **fresh parsley**

4 cups **penne pasta** (about 12 oz/340 g)

4 cups **broccoli florets**

2 cups shredded **Fontina cheese**

½ cup grated **Parmesan cheese**

In large skillet, heat half of the oil over medium-high heat; sauté sausage until browned, about 8 minutes. Using slotted spoon, transfer to bowl.

Drain fat from pan; add remaining oil. Cook onions, garlic, Italian herb seasoning and pepper over medium heat, stirring occasionally, until softened, about 5 minutes.

Add tomatoes and tomato paste, mashing with potato masher to break up; bring to boil. Return sausage to pan; reduce heat and simmer until thickened, about 15 minutes. Stir in parsley.

Meanwhile, in large saucepan of boiling lightly salted water, cook pasta for 7 minutes. Add broccoli; cook until tender-crisp and pasta is al dente, 1 minute. Drain and return to pot. Add sauce; toss to coat. Transfer to 12-cup (3 L) oval baking dish. *(Make-ahead: Let cool for 30 minutes. Cover and refrigerate for up to 24 hours; add 10 minutes to baking time.)*

Sprinkle with Fontina and Parmesan cheeses. Bake in 375°F (190°C) oven until bubbly, about 30 minutes.

Makes 8 servings. PER SERVING: about 439 cal, 24 g pro, 19 g total fat (9 g sat. fat), 45 g carb, 5 g fibre, 61 mg chol, 1,060 mg sodium, 588 mg potassium. % RDI: 28% calcium, 54% iron, 27% vit A, 87% vit C, 55% folate.

SPINACH, RADICCHIO & RADISH SALAD

Boston lettuce and baby spinach have a pleasing mild taste that tempers the somewhat bitter radicchio. Spicy radishes and a tarragon vinaigrette put the perfect finishing touch on this nice-enough-for-company salad. It's easily doubled for a larger group.

In salad bowl, toss together lettuce, spinach, radicchio and radishes.

Whisk together oil, vinegar, salt, pepper and sugar; pour over greens and toss to coat.

2 cups torn **Boston lettuce** or Bibb lettuce

2 cups **fresh baby spinach**

1 cup torn **radicchio**

4 **radishes,** thinly sliced

2 tbsp **extra-virgin olive oil**

4 tsp **tarragon vinegar** or white wine vinegar

¼ tsp each **salt** and **pepper**

Pinch **granulated sugar**

Healthy bonus: Spinach is packed with all sorts of beneficial nutrients. It provides vitamins A, C and K, and has a reputation as a superfood due to its high antioxidant content. Tender fresh baby spinach leaves are tasty in salads (those young stems and veins are edible and don't need to be torn out, like the ones in mature spinach leaves). Baby spinach is also great to keep in the refrigerator to add to soups, stir-fries or your morning omelette.

Makes 4 servings. PER SERVING: about 72 cal, 1 g pro, 7 g total fat (1 g sat. fat), 2 g carb, 1 g fibre, 0 mg chol, 160 mg sodium. % RDI: 3% calcium, 6% iron, 18% vit A, 12% vit C, 23% folate.

BEEF TACOS WITH CORN SALSA

OK, who doesn't love tacos? This go-to beef version with its savoury homemade corn salsa is a real crowd-pleaser and a family favourite. Double or triple the recipe for a party.

1 tsp **vegetable oil**

1 cup chopped **onion**

2 cloves **garlic,** chopped

12 oz (340 g) **extra-lean ground beef**

2 tbsp **tomato paste**

2 tsp **chili powder**

¼ tsp each **salt** and **pepper**

1 **avocado,** pitted, peeled and diced

1 cup **frozen corn kernels,** cooked and cooled

½ cup **cherry tomatoes,** quartered

1 **green onion,** sliced

1 tsp each grated **lime zest** and **lime juice**

8 small **flour tortillas** (6 inches/ 15 cm)

¼ cup **sour cream**

⅓ cup shredded **Cheddar cheese**

In nonstick skillet, heat oil over medium heat; cook onion, stirring occasionally, until softened, 4 to 5 minutes. Add garlic; cook for 1 minute.

Add beef; cook, breaking up with spoon, until no longer pink, about 5 minutes. Stir in tomato paste, chili powder and half each of the salt and pepper. Remove from heat and keep warm.

Meanwhile, toss together avocado, corn, tomatoes, green onion, lime zest, lime juice and remaining salt and pepper. Set aside.

Heat tortillas according to package directions. Divide beef mixture among tortillas; top each with corn salsa, sour cream and Cheddar cheese.

Makes 4 servings. PER SERVING: about 521 cal, 29 g pro, 25 g total fat (8 g sat. fat), 50 g carb, 7 g fibre, 62 mg chol, 725 mg sodium, 923 mg potassium. % RDI: 11% calcium, 31% iron, 13% vit A, 28% vit C, 61% folate.

MEDITERRANEAN PORK & VEGETABLE MEAT LOAF

Slice and serve this veggie-studded meat loaf hot with mashed potatoes or buttered orzo. If there's any left over, turn cold slices into the most delectable sandwiches you can imagine.

1 **onion**

1 **zucchini** (unpeeled)

1 tbsp **extra-virgin olive oil**

½ cup finely diced **sweet red pepper**

2 cloves **garlic,** minced

2 **eggs**

⅔ cup **tomato sauce**

1 cup shredded **Fontina cheese**

½ cup **fresh bread crumbs**

2 tsp **wine vinegar**

1 tsp **dried marjoram** or oregano

½ tsp each **salt** and **pepper**

¼ tsp **hot pepper flakes** (optional)

1¼ lb (565 g) **lean ground pork**

Coarsely grate onion and zucchini; squeeze out moisture.

In skillet, heat oil over medium heat; fry onion, zucchini, red pepper and garlic, stirring occasionally, until softened, about 10 minutes. Let cool.

Meanwhile, in large bowl, whisk together eggs, ¼ cup of the tomato sauce, the Fontina cheese, bread crumbs, vinegar, marjoram, salt, pepper, and hot pepper flakes (if using); mix in pork and vegetable mixture. Pat evenly into 9- x 5-inch (2 L) loaf pan.

Bake in 350°F (180°C) oven until golden, about 1 hour. Drain off fat; spread remaining tomato sauce over top. Bake until instant-read thermometer inserted in centre reads 160°F (71°C), about 30 minutes.

Any ground meat or poultry is delicious in meat loaves. A tasty base recipe like this one makes it easy to improvise. Try one type of meat or create a signature mix – how about beef, pork *and* veal? Mmmmm.

Makes 6 to 8 servings. PER EACH OF 8 SERVINGS: about 233 cal, 19 g pro, 15 g total fat (6 g sat. fat), 6 g carb, 1 g fibre, 108 mg chol, 431 mg sodium. % RDI: 10% calcium, 10% iron, 12% vit A, 30% vit C, 10% folate.

MEXICAN MEAT LOAVES

These little gems are easy to make and don't require as long a cooking time as a larger single loaf. Serve with rice, corn and a quick avocado salad.

In large skillet, heat oil over medium heat; cook onion, stirring occasionally, until softened and golden, about 4 minutes. Stir in garlic, oregano, cumin, allspice, salt and pepper; cook for 1 minute. Transfer to plate; let cool.

In small bowl, stir ketchup with chipotle peppers; set aside.

In large bowl, whisk eggs; mix in bread crumbs, green onions, yogurt, beef, onion mixture and all but ¼ cup of the ketchup mixture.

Form into three 7-inch (18 cm) long logs; place on parchment paper–lined rimmed baking sheet.

Bake in 375°F (190°C) oven until instant-read thermometer inserted in loaves reads 160°F (71°C), about 25 minutes. Spoon remaining ketchup mixture over top.

1 tbsp **vegetable oil**

1 **onion,** finely chopped

2 cloves **garlic,** minced

1 tsp each **dried oregano** and **ground cumin**

½ tsp each **ground allspice, salt** and **pepper**

⅔ cup **ketchup**

2 tbsp **canned chipotle peppers in adobo sauce,** minced

3 **eggs**

½ cup **fresh bread crumbs**

½ cup chopped **green onions**

½ cup **Balkan-style plain yogurt**

2 lb (900 g) **medium ground beef**

Makes 6 to 8 servings. PER EACH OF 8 SERVINGS: about 309 cal, 25 g pro, 18 g total fat (7 g sat. fat), 11 g carb, 1 g fibre, 135 mg chol, 504 mg sodium, 443 mg potassium. % RDI: w6% calcium, 20% iron, 8% vit A, 7% vit C, 11% folate.

ITALIAN MEAT LOAF

Soaking the bread crumbs in milk keeps this vibrantly flavoured Italian-style loaf moist and succulent. If you have cheese fiends at the table, sprinkle more shredded provolone over the top during the last 10 minutes of cooking.

Stir bread crumbs with milk; let stand for 10 minutes.

Meanwhile, in skillet, heat oil over medium heat; cook onion, stirring occasionally, until golden, about 6 minutes. Stir in garlic and oregano; cook for 2 minutes.

In large bowl, mix together veal, pork, sun-dried tomatoes, eggs, parsley, Parmesan cheese, olives, salt, pepper, bread crumb mixture and onion mixture. Press half into greased 9- x 5-inch (2 L) loaf pan. Sprinkle with provolone cheese. Press remaining meat mixture evenly over top.

Bake in 350°F (180°C) oven until instant-read thermometer inserted in centre reads 160°F (71°C), 60 to 70 minutes. Drain off any fat. Let stand for 5 to 10 minutes before slicing. *(Make-ahead: Refrigerate in airtight container for up to 3 days.)*

1¼ cups **fresh bread crumbs**

½ cup **milk**

4 tsp **olive oil**

1½ cups chopped **onion**

2 cloves **garlic,** minced

1 tsp **dried oregano**

1 lb (450 g) **ground veal**

1 lb (450 g) **lean ground pork**

½ cup drained **oil-packed sun-dried tomatoes,** finely chopped

2 **eggs**

½ cup chopped **fresh parsley**

½ cup grated **Parmesan cheese**

⅓ cup chopped **green olives**

½ tsp each **salt** and **pepper**

¾ cup shredded **provolone cheese**

Makes 8 servings. PER SERVING: about 355 cal, 30 g pro, 21 g total fat (8 g sat. fat), 10 g carb, 1 g fibre, 142 mg chol, 567 mg sodium. % RDI: 20% calcium, 15% iron, 10% vit A, 23% vit C, 15% folate.

CHOPS, STEAKS

& RIBS

RECIPES

PARMESAN-CRUSTED VEAL SANDWICHES

Deliciously crusty veal and creamy caper mayo are a match made in culinary heaven. This sandwich is less of an everyday affair and more of a meal to remember.

2 **eggs**

¾ cup grated **Parmesan cheese**

½ cup chopped **fresh parsley**

4 **veal cutlets** or pork cutlets (12 oz/340 g total)

½ tsp **pepper**

¼ cup **all-purpose flour**

1 cup **fresh bread crumbs**

¼ cup **vegetable oil**

4 **soft buns,** halved

2 cups trimmed **arugula** or watercress

CAPER MAYO:

⅓ cup **mayonnaise**

1 tbsp **capers** (with liquid), chopped

CAPER MAYO: Stir mayonnaise with capers and liquid.

In large bowl, whisk eggs with 2 tbsp water; whisk in Parmesan cheese and parsley.

Between plastic wrap, pound veal to scant ¼-inch (5 mm) thickness. Sprinkle with pepper. Place flour and bread crumbs in separate shallow dishes. Dip veal into flour, turning to coat; shake off excess. Dip into egg mixture. Dip into bread crumbs, turning to coat.

In skillet, heat half of the oil over medium-high heat; cook half of the veal until browned and just a hint of pink remains inside, about 5 minutes. Repeat with remaining oil and veal.

Spread caper mayo over cut sides of buns; sandwich veal and arugula in buns.

Fresh bread crumbs are a cinch to make: Cut up crusty bread – day-old, slightly hard baguettes work really well – and whirl in the food processor until in crumbs. Try whole wheat for a fibre and flavour boost.

Makes 4 sandwiches. PER SANDWICH: about 652 cal, 35 g pro, 39 g total fat (8 g sat. fat), 38 g carb, 2 g fibre, 162 mg chol, 845 mg sodium, 520 mg potassium. % RDI: 30% calcium, 30% iron, 17% vit A, 17% vit C, 55% folate.

VIETNAMESE SANDWICH (BEEF BÁNH MÌ)

A bánh mì is a crusty French-style bun stuffed with a classic explosion of Vietnamese flavours and textures – sweet and sour, crunchy and soft. We've switched the traditional grilled pork filling for lean flank steak, and used readily available liverwurst instead of the typical Vietnamese pâté.

4 **crusty French-style sandwich rolls,** halved lengthwise

¼ cup **mayonnaise**

⅓ cup **liverwurst**

Half **English cucumber,** cut in sticks

12 sprigs **fresh cilantro**

1 **red finger hot pepper** (optional), thinly sliced

MARINATED FLANK STEAK:

2 tbsp **fish sauce**

2 tbsp **vegetable oil**

1 tbsp **granulated sugar**

2 tsp **sesame oil**

1 clove **garlic,** minced

¼ tsp **pepper**

1 lb (450 g) **beef flank marinating steak**

PICKLED CARROT & DAIKON:

1 **carrot,** julienned

4 oz (115 g) **daikon radish,** julienned

2 tbsp **granulated sugar**

½ tsp **salt**

¼ cup **unseasoned rice vinegar**

MARINATED FLANK STEAK: In shallow dish, whisk together fish sauce, vegetable oil, sugar, sesame oil, garlic and pepper; add steak, turning to coat. Cover and refrigerate for 30 minutes. *(Make-ahead: Refrigerate for up to 24 hours.)*

PICKLED CARROT & DAIKON: Meanwhile, in bowl, toss together carrot, radish, 1 tbsp of the sugar and half of the salt; let stand until softened and pliable, about 10 minutes. Rinse under cold water; drain and return to bowl. Whisk together vinegar and remaining sugar and salt; let stand until dissolved. Pour over carrot mixture; cover and refrigerate, stirring once, for 1 hour. *(Make-ahead: Refrigerate for up to 2 days.)* Drain well.

Drain steak; discard marinade. In large ovenproof skillet, sear steak over medium-high heat for 2 minutes per side. Transfer to 400°F (200°C) oven; cook until medium-rare, 5 to 8 minutes. *(Make-ahead: Let cool slightly. Cover and refrigerate for up to 24 hours.)* Transfer to cutting board and tent with foil; let stand for 5 minutes before thinly slicing across the grain.

Spread cut sides of rolls with mayonnaise; spread liverwurst over bottom halves. Sandwich steak, cucumber, carrot mixture, cilantro, and hot pepper (if using) in buns.

Makes 4 sandwiches. PER SANDWICH: about 551 cal, 31 g pro, 29 g total fat (7 g sat. fat), 40 g carb, 4 g fibre, 75 mg chol, 1,050 mg sodium, 527 mg potassium. % RDI: 8% calcium, 39% iron, 107% vit A, 17% vit C, 41% folate.

VIETNAMESE COFFEE

Nothing goes better with delicious Vietnamese food – like our Vietnamese Sandwich (opposite) – than the country's signature iced coffee. Sweetened with condensed milk, it definitely heads toward dessert territory, but it's a wonderfully cool, summery treat.

Place sweetened condensed milk in tall glass. Spoon ground coffee into French press; pour in boiling water.

Cover and let stand for 5 minutes. Press filter down; pour coffee over milk in glass. (Or use a Vietnamese-style drip filter: Place filter on top of glass; spoon in coffee. Slowly pour in boiling water to prevent from streaming through too quickly; cover and let drip for 5 minutes.)

Add ice to glass; stir to chill and incorporate condensed milk.

1 tbsp **sweetened condensed milk** (or to taste)
1 tbsp **coarsely ground coffee**
⅔ cup **boiling water**
Ice cubes

TIP

The most authentic coffee for this delicious drink contains chicory in addition to coffee beans, such as Café du Monde. A good French roast coffee is another excellent alternative. A coarse grind works best in the French press.

Makes 1 serving. PER SERVING: about 62 cal, 2 g pro, 2 g total fat (1 g sat. fat), 10 g carb, 0 g fibre, 7 mg chol, 27 mg sodium, 129 mg potassium. % RDI: 5% calcium, 1% vit A, 2% folate

CEMITA-STYLE PORK SANDWICH

This popular Latin-style street food is traditionally served on a bun called a cemita, which is sesame-topped egg bread. Here, we use challah, which is similar to cemita and more readily available. Marinating in spices and lime juice gives the meat a zesty kick, which is offset by a cool guacamole spread.

In bowl, combine half of the lime juice, the chipotle pepper, adobo sauce, oregano, cumin, coriander, salt and pepper. Add pork, turning to coat. Cover and refrigerate for 1 hour. *(Make-ahead: Refrigerate for up to 24 hours.)*

Peel, pit and chop avocado. In bowl, mash avocado with fork; mix in cilantro and remaining lime juice. Set aside.

Weave pork slices onto 4 metal or soaked wooden skewers. Grill, covered, on greased grill over medium-high heat, turning occasionally, until juices run clear when pork is pierced and just a hint of pink remains inside, 8 to 10 minutes. Remove skewers.

Spread avocado mixture on cut sides of bun tops; sandwich lettuce, tomatoes, pork and onion in buns.

2 tbsp **lime juice**

1 **canned chipotle pepper in adobo sauce,** finely chopped

1 tsp **adobo sauce**

½ tsp **dried oregano**

¼ tsp each **ground cumin** and **ground coriander**

¼ tsp each **salt** and **pepper**

1 lb (450 g) **pork tenderloin,** sliced ¼ inch (5 mm) thick

1 **avocado**

2 tbsp chopped **fresh cilantro**

4 round **challah buns** or sesame hamburger buns, halved

8 leaves **Boston lettuce**

2 small **tomatoes,** thinly sliced

½ cup thinly sliced **red onion**

Makes 4 sandwiches. PER SANDWICH: about 453 cal, 34 g pro, 15 g total fat (3 g sat. fat), 46 g carb, 6 g fibre, 101 mg chol, 620 mg sodium, 868 mg potassium. % RDI: 10% calcium, 31% iron, 15% vit A, 25% vit C, 56% folate.

PORK SANDWICHES WITH ASIAN MANGO SLAW

The crusty rolls absorb just the right amount of dressing from the tangy-sweet slaw to be flavourful but not soggy. If you like more heat, top with a little more sriracha.

4 **crusty rolls,** halved and toasted

4 **boneless fast-fry pork chops**
  (1 lb/450 g)

Pinch each **salt** and **pepper**

2 tsp **vegetable oil**

MANGO SLAW:

2 tbsp **unseasoned rice vinegar**

2 tsp **granulated sugar**

1 tsp **sesame oil**

½ tsp **salt**

Pinch **hot pepper flakes** (optional)

3 cups thinly sliced **napa cabbage**

1 **ripe mango,** peeled, pitted and
  sliced in thin strips

Half **sweet red pepper,** thinly sliced

SPICY MAYO:

¼ cup **light mayonnaise**

1 tsp each **unseasoned rice vinegar**
  and **sriracha**

MANGO SLAW: In large bowl, whisk together vinegar, sugar, oil, salt, and hot pepper flakes (if using) until sugar is dissolved. Add cabbage, mango and red pepper; toss together to coat.

SPICY MAYO: Whisk together mayonnaise, vinegar and sriracha; spread over cut sides of rolls.

Sprinkle pork with salt and pepper. In large skillet, heat half of the oil over medium-high heat; cook half of the pork, turning once, until lightly browned and juices run clear when pork is pierced, about 2 minutes. Repeat with remaining oil and pork.

Sandwich pork and slaw in rolls.

Makes 4 sandwiches. PER SANDWICH: about 490 cal, 32 g pro, 19 g total fat (4 g sat. fat), 49 g carb, 3 g fibre, 65 mg chol, 797 mg sodium, 641 mg potassium. % RDI: 11% calcium, 21% iron, 11% vit A, 98% vit C, 50% folate.

SPANISH-STYLE LAMB KABOBS WITH RED ONION SALSA

**For a casual dinner, cube the lamb; you can grill (or broil) these skewers in about 10 minutes.
For company, leave the leg whole and carve at the table (see the variation that follows).**

Trim any fat from lamb; cut lamb into 2-inch (5 cm) cubes to make about 48 pieces. Toss together lamb, oil, paprika and cumin. Cover and refrigerate for 4 hours. *(Make-ahead: Refrigerate for up to 24 hours.)*

Thread about 6 cubes of lamb onto each of 8 metal skewers. Sprinkle with salt. Grill, covered, on greased grill over medium-high heat, turning once, until browned but still slightly pink inside, 10 to 12 minutes.

RED ONION SALSA: Meanwhile, stir together onion, tomatoes, garlic, oil, vinegar, basil, salt and pepper. Serve with lamb.

CHANGE IT UP
Spanish-Style Butterflied Leg of Lamb With Red Onion Salsa

Marinate lamb leg whole. Grill over medium-high heat or roast in 425°F (220°C) oven until instant read thermometer reads 145°F (63°C) for medium-rare, 25 to 35 minutes. Transfer to cutting board and tent with foil; let stand for 10 minutes before thinly slicing across the grain. Pour any juices over slices. Serve with salsa.

Makes 6 to 8 servings.

3 lb (1.35 kg) **boneless butterflied leg of lamb**

3 tbsp **extra-virgin olive oil**

4 tsp **smoked paprika** or sweet paprika

2 tsp **ground cumin**

1 tsp **sea salt** or salt

RED ONION SALSA:

1½ cups thinly sliced **red onion** (about 1 medium)

2 **plum tomatoes,** seeded and cut in ½-inch (1 cm) wide strips

1 clove **garlic,** minced

2 tbsp **extra-virgin olive oil**

2 tbsp **red wine vinegar**

6 leaves **fresh basil,** torn

¼ tsp each **salt** and **pepper**

Makes 8 servings. PER SERVING: about 325 cal, 36 g pro, 18 g total fat (5 g sat. fat), 4 g carb, 1 g fibre, 128 mg chol, 421 mg sodium. % RDI: 2% calcium, 26% iron, 8% vit A, 10% vit C, 5% folate.

PORK TACOS WITH RED CABBAGE SLAW & GUACAMOLE

Simple guacamole is the perfect complement to juicy pork tenderloin and a crunchy slaw. To prevent browning when you make the guacamole in advance, leave the avocado pit in the mashed flesh and place plastic wrap directly on the surface; remove the pit right before serving.

1 tsp each **smoked paprika** and **chili powder**

½ tsp **ground coriander**

1 lb (450 g) **pork tenderloin**

8 small **whole grain whole wheat tortillas** (6 inches/15 cm)

⅓ cup chopped **fresh cilantro**

RED CABBAGE SLAW:

2½ cups finely shredded **red cabbage**

¼ cup **Greek yogurt**

1 tsp **lime juice**

½ tsp **liquid honey**

½ tsp **cider vinegar**

Pinch each **salt** and **pepper**

GUACAMOLE:

1 **ripe avocado,** pitted and peeled

1 tbsp **lime juice**

¼ tsp **pepper**

Pinch each **salt** and **smoked paprika**

1 clove **garlic,** minced

In bowl, mix together paprika, chili powder and coriander; rub all over pork. Line baking sheet with foil; grease foil. Add pork; bake in 400°F (200°C) oven, turning once, until juices run clear when pork is pierced and instant-read thermometer inserted in thickest part reads 160°F (71°C), about 20 minutes.

Transfer pork to cutting board; tent with foil. Let stand for 10 minutes before cutting into ½-inch (1 cm) thick slices.

RED CABBAGE SLAW: Meanwhile, toss together cabbage, yogurt, lime juice, honey, vinegar, salt and pepper.

GUACAMOLE: In bowl, mash avocado and lime juice with fork. Stir in pepper, salt, paprika and garlic.

Heat tortillas according to package directions. Spread guacamole over tortillas; top with pork, red cabbage slaw and cilantro.

Makes 4 servings. PER SERVING: about 451 cal, 36 g pro, 16 g total fat (4 g sat. fat), 40 g carb, 9 g fibre, 67 mg chol, 578 mg sodium, 1,043 mg potassium. % RDI: 7% calcium, 22% iron, 7% vit A, 53% vit C, 39% folate.

BEEF MILANESE WITH FENNEL SLAW

Spices, rather than salt, flavour the crispy crust on these sodium-wise tender beef cutlets. Uncooked thinly sliced beef is labelled as sandwich-cut or fast-fry steaks. Use a mandoline or the slicing attachment of your food processor to cut the fennel and red onion quickly.

1 tsp each **garlic powder** and **onion powder**

¼ tsp **pepper**

10 oz (280 g) **beef inside round sandwich steaks** or beef top sirloin sandwich steaks

1 cup **panko**

¼ cup **all-purpose flour**

2 **eggs,** lightly beaten

2 tbsp **olive oil**

1 **lemon,** cut in wedges

FENNEL SLAW:
3 tbsp **extra-virgin olive oil**

3 tbsp **lemon juice**

1 tsp **liquid honey**

1 tsp **Dijon mustard**

½ tsp **pepper**

Pinch **salt**

1 bulb **fennel**

1 **carrot,** shredded

½ cup thinly sliced **red onion**

¼ cup chopped **fresh parsley**

FENNEL SLAW: In large bowl, whisk together oil, lemon juice, honey, mustard, pepper and salt. Remove fennel tops; slice bulb thinly. Add fennel, carrot, onion and parsley to dressing; toss to combine. Let stand for 20 minutes.

Meanwhile, combine garlic powder, onion powder and pepper; sprinkle over steaks. Pour panko and flour into separate shallow dishes. Beat eggs with 2 tsp water. One at a time, dip steaks into flour, shaking off excess; dip into eggs. Dredge in panko, pressing to adhere.

In large nonstick skillet, heat 1 tbsp of the oil over medium-high heat; cook steaks in 2 batches, adding remaining oil as necessary and turning once, until golden, about 3 minutes. Serve with slaw and lemon wedges.

Makes 4 servings. PER SERVING: about 351 cal, 20 g pro, 21 g total fat (4 g sat. fat), 22 g carb, 3 g fibre, 97 mg chol, 130 mg sodium, 560 mg potassium. % RDI: 5% calcium, 19% iron, 28% vit A, 33% vit C, 19% folate.

SESAME BEEF SALAD

**This cold noodle salad is lovely served with hot flank steak for dinner.
On another night, try serving the noodles with sautéed shrimp or grilled chicken.**

Sprinkle steak with salt and pepper. In large skillet, heat vegetable oil over medium heat; cook steak, turning once, until medium-rare, 10 to 12 minutes. Tent with foil; let stand for 10 minutes. Slice across the grain into ½-inch (1 cm) thick slices.

Meanwhile, cook noodles according to package directions. Rinse under cold water until cool; drain.

Using vegetable peeler, cut carrots into long thin strips. In large bowl, combine carrots, green onions, cilantro, peanuts and noodles.

Whisk together rice vinegar, sesame oil, soy sauce and ginger; pour over noodles. Toss to coat. Arrange steak slices over top.

12 oz (340 g) **beef flank marinating steak**

Pinch each **salt** and **pepper**

2 tsp **vegetable oil**

6 oz (170 g) **rice stick vermicelli** (about ⅛ inch/3 mm wide)

2 **carrots**

3 **green onions,** sliced

⅓ cup chopped **fresh cilantro**

¼ cup coarsely chopped **unsalted roasted peanuts**

3 tbsp **unseasoned rice vinegar**

2 tbsp **sesame oil**

2 tbsp **sodium-reduced soy sauce**

2 tsp grated **fresh ginger**

TIP

Rice vinegar comes in seasoned and unseasoned varieties. Seasoned contains sugar and salt in addition to the vinegar – perfect for flavouring sushi rice or adding to some recipes. Unseasoned is just straight-up vinegar, which works in dressings, marinades and much more.

Makes 4 servings. PER SERVING: about 428 cal, 22 g pro, 18 g total fat (4 g sat. fat), 43 g carb, 3 g fibre, 36 mg chol, 388 mg sodium, 420 mg potassium. % RDI: 4% calcium, 16% iron, 51% vit A, 8% vit C, 16% folate.

STEAK TACOS WITH PEBRE SALSA

With a salsa inspired by the traditional Chilean pebre (Spanish for "pepper") sauce,
these steak tacos are equally delicious when made with chicken breasts. Our version is mild, so if you
like a little heat, add 1 tbsp minced jalapeño pepper to the salsa.

In skillet, heat oil over medium heat; cook steak, turning once, until medium-rare, 6 to 8 minutes. Let stand for 10 minutes; slice across the grain.

SALSA: Meanwhile, in food processor, purée together cilantro, parsley, garlic, onion, oil, vinegar, salt and pepper.

Heat tortillas according to package directions. Divide steak among tortillas; top with salsa, tomatoes and lettuce.

2 tsp **vegetable oil**

12 oz (340 g) **beef top sirloin grilling steak**

8 small **whole grain whole wheat tortillas** (6 inches/15 cm)

½ cup **cherry tomatoes,** halved

1 cup shredded **Boston lettuce** or other lettuce

SALSA:

1 cup packed **fresh cilantro**

1 cup packed **fresh parsley**

1 clove **garlic,** chopped

¼ cup chopped **red onion**

2 tbsp **olive oil**

2 tsp **red wine vinegar**

¼ tsp each **salt** and **pepper**

Makes 4 servings. PER SERVING: about 399 cal, 26 g pro, 18 g total fat (4 g sat. fat), 33 g carb, 5 g fibre, 40 mg chol, 690 mg sodium, 662 mg potassium. % RDI: 3% calcium, 29% iron, 22% vit A, 42% vit C, 32% folate.

GINGER BEER

This nonalcoholic beer is a must-drink in the Caribbean, where each cook seems to have his or her own recipe. This one is sweet with a spicy, slightly effervescent bite – perfectly refreshing served over ice or transformed into a Dark & Stormy cocktail (below). Either way, it's totally tasty with jerk dishes.

1½ cups **granulated sugar**
½ cup grated **fresh ginger**
2 tbsp **lime juice**
4 cups **boiling water**
½ cup **warm water**
½ tsp **active dry yeast**

In large heatproof bowl, stir together sugar, ginger and lime juice; pour in boiling water, stirring until sugar is dissolved. Let cool to lukewarm (about 100°F/38°C), 20 minutes.

Meanwhile, stir warm water with yeast; let stand until frothy, about 10 minutes. Stir into ginger mixture.

Cover and let stand at room temperature for 24 hours. Strain through cheesecloth-lined sieve into airtight jar. Seal and refrigerate until cold. *(Make-ahead: Refrigerate for up to 2 days.)*

CHANGE IT UP
Dark & Stormy

Fill highball glass with ice. Add 2 oz (¼ cup) dark rum and ¾ cup Ginger Beer. Squeeze wedge of lime over top and drop into drink. Stir to combine.

Makes 1 serving.

 Grated, not chopped, ginger is right for this drink, because the tiny pieces infuse their flavours into the liquid more readily. A rasp is the perfect tool for the job.

Makes 4 servings. PER SERVING: about 311.cal, 1 g pro, trace total fat (trace sat. fat), 80 g carb, trace fibre, 0 mg chol, 10 mg sodium. % RDI: 1% calcium, 2% iron, 3% vit C, 7% folate.

JERK BEEF SALAD WITH GRILLED PEPPERS

Jerk seasoning is a convenient ingredient to keep on hand during grilling season. It gives meat and poultry a wonderful kick that captures the essence of Caribbean cuisine. Treat yourself to a spicy homemade Ginger Beer (opposite) when you sit down to eat this brightly flavoured and coloured salad.

In shallow bowl, whisk together 3 tbsp of the oil, the lime juice, jerk seasoning and soy sauce. Remove 2 tbsp and set aside.

Add steak to bowl and turn to coat. Let stand for 15 minutes. *(Make-ahead: Cover and refrigerate steak and reserved marinade separately for up to 8 hours.)*

Grill steak, covered, on greased grill over medium heat, turning once, until medium-rare, 10 to 12 minutes. Transfer to cutting board and tent with foil; let stand for 10 minutes before thinly slicing across the grain.

Meanwhile, halve and seed red, green and yellow peppers; cut each half into 3 pieces. Cut onion into ½-inch (1 cm) thick slices. Brush peppers and onion with remaining oil; sprinkle with salt and pepper. Grill, covered and turning once, until softened, 12 to 15 minutes. Separate onion into rings.

In large bowl, toss greens with reserved marinade. Arrange on 4 plates. Top with peppers, onion and steak.

¼ cup **extra-virgin olive oil**

4 tsp **lime juice**

2 tsp **jerk seasoning**

1 tsp **soy sauce**

1 lb (450 g) **beef flank marinating steak**

1 each **sweet red pepper, sweet green pepper** and **sweet yellow pepper**

1 small **red onion**

¼ tsp each **salt** and **pepper**

8 cups torn **mixed greens**

Makes 4 servings. PER SERVING: about 355 cal, 29 g pro, 23 g total fat (6 g sat. fat), 10 g carb, 3 g fibre, 46 mg chol, 509 mg sodium. % RDI: 8% calcium, 23% iron, 36% vit A, 218% vit C, 32% folate.

STEAK FRITES

It's hard to find a French bistro menu that doesn't serve up classic steak frites (or fries). Letting the steak rest after cooking keeps it juicy by allowing the juices to redistribute throughout the meat.

1½ lb (675 g) **yellow-fleshed potatoes,** scrubbed

1 tbsp **olive oil**

¼ tsp each **salt** and **pepper**

1 lb (450 g) **beef sirloin grilling steak,** cut in 4 portions

2 tsp chopped **fresh thyme**

⅓ cup **mayonnaise**

1 tbsp chopped **fresh chives**

2 tsp **Dijon mustard**

1 tsp **lemon juice**

Cut potatoes into ½-inch (1 cm) thick wedges; toss with half each of the oil, salt and pepper. Spread on parchment paper–lined baking sheet; bake in 450°F (230°C) oven, turning once, until tender, about 30 minutes. Broil until golden, about 3 minutes.

Meanwhile, sprinkle steak with thyme and remaining salt and pepper. In skillet, heat remaining oil over medium-high heat; cook steak, turning once, until medium-rare, about 6 minutes. Transfer to cutting board and tent with foil; let stand for 10 minutes.

Stir together mayonnaise, chives, mustard and lemon juice. Serve alongside steak as dipping sauce for potato wedges.

Makes 4 servings. PER SERVING: about 412 cal, 26 g pro, 23 g total fat (5 g sat. fat), 26 g carb, 2 g fibre, 60 mg chol, 333 mg sodium, 1,047 mg potassium. % RDI: 2% calcium, 25% iron, 2% vit A, 37% vit C, 10% folate.

MEXICAN-STYLE RIB EYE STEAKS & PEPPERS

**Oregano, cumin and coriander make these juicy steaks savoury, not spicy.
Serve with warm corn tortillas and wrap up the beef and peppers to make tasty soft tacos.**

2 tbsp **extra-virgin olive oil**

2 cloves **garlic,** minced

1 tsp each **pepper** and **dried oregano**

¾ tsp **salt**

½ tsp each **ground cumin** and
ground coriander

4 **beef rib eye grilling medallions,**
about 1½ inches (4 cm) thick

2 each **sweet green peppers** and
sweet red peppers

In bowl, combine 4 tsp of the oil, the garlic, pepper, oregano, salt, cumin and coriander. Add beef, turning and rubbing to coat. Cover and let stand for 15 minutes.

Meanwhile, grill green and red peppers, covered, on greased grill over medium-high heat, turning often, until charred and tender, 15 to 20 minutes. Let cool enough to handle. Peel, core and seed peppers; cut into quarters and toss with remaining oil.

Add beef to grill; grill, covered and turning once, until medium-rare, about 10 minutes. Transfer to platter; tent with foil. Let stand for 5 minutes before serving with peppers.

Makes 4 servings. PER SERVING: about 342 cal, 25 g pro, 23 g total fat (8 g sat. fat), 9 g carb, 2 g fibre, 60 mg chol, 481 mg sodium. % RDI: 3% calcium, 29% iron, 23% vit A, 235% vit C, 11% folate.

PORK KATSU

**In Japanese, *tonkatsu* means a deep-fried breaded pork cutlet,
which is traditionally served with a sweet, slightly spicy sauce. Steamed short-grain rice
and a shredded cabbage salad are the perfect partners.**

Place pork between plastic wrap; pound with meat mallet to about ½-inch (1 cm) thickness. Sprinkle with salt and pepper.

Whisk egg with 1 tbsp water. Place flour and panko in separate shallow dishes. Dip pork into flour to coat; shake off excess. Dip into egg mixture, letting excess drip off. Dip into panko, patting to coat evenly.

In deep skillet, heat 1 inch (2.5 cm) oil over medium heat; cook pork, in batches, until juices run clear when pork is pierced and just a hint of pink remains inside, 6 to 8 minutes.

Meanwhile, whisk ketchup with Worcestershire sauce. Serve with pork.

4 **boneless pork loin chops**
(1½ lb/675 g total)
¼ tsp each **salt** and **pepper**
1 **egg**
2 tbsp **all-purpose flour**
1½ cups **panko**
Vegetable oil for frying
¼ cup **ketchup**
2 tbsp **Worcestershire sauce**

If you don't feel like making homemade sauce and can make it to an Asian market, commercial tonkatsu sauce – such as Bulldog brand – is a handy option for these cutlets.

Makes 4 to 6 servings. PER EACH OF 6 SERVINGS: about 281 cal, 27 g pro, 14 g total fat (4 g sat. fat), 11 g carb, 1 g fibre, 92 mg chol, 340 mg sodium, 485 mg potassium. % RDI: 2% calcium, 11% iron, 2% vit A, 5% vit C, 7% folate.

WHITE BEAN SALAD WITH SEARED STEAK

**Creamy white beans are a delicious base for a satisfying dinner salad.
With quick-cooking grilling medallions, this dish comes together
in minutes – perfect for a busy weeknight.**

Sprinkle steak with half of the thyme and the salt and pepper. In cast-iron or nonstick skillet, heat vegetable oil over medium-high heat; cook steak, turning once, until medium-rare, 6 to 8 minutes.

Transfer steak to platter; let stand for 5 minutes.

Meanwhile, in large bowl, whisk together olive oil, vinegar and Dijon mustard; stir in beans, cucumber, feta cheese, onion and remaining thyme. Serve with steak.

4 **beef top sirloin grilling medallions** (about 1 lb/450 g total)

1 tbsp chopped **fresh thyme**

Pinch each **salt** and **pepper**

1 tsp **vegetable oil**

2 tbsp **extra-virgin olive oil**

2 tbsp **red wine vinegar**

1 tbsp **Dijon mustard**

2 cans (19 oz/540 mL each) **white kidney beans,** drained and rinsed

Half **English cucumber,** chopped

½ cup cubed **feta cheese**

¼ cup diced **red onion**

Makes 4 servings. PER SERVING: about 468 cal, 38 g pro, 18 g total fat (6 g sat. fat), 38 g carb, 15 g fibre, 70 mg chol, 919 mg sodium, 852 mg potassium. % RDI: 17% calcium, 36% iron, 3% vit A, 8% vit C, 41% folate.

GRILLED FOUR-PEPPERCORN T-BONES

Good-quality steaks, peppercorns, garlic, sea salt and olive oil are all you need for this simple yet spectacular dish. Using a mélange of pepper makes the steaks more interesting – the robust hit of one type of pepper complements the fruitiness of another.

¼ cup **extra-virgin olive oil**

2 tbsp **mixed peppercorn medley,** coarsely ground

2 cloves **garlic,** minced

2 **beef T-bone grilling steaks** (about 2 lb/900 g total), 1½ inches (4 cm) thick

1½ tsp **sea salt**

Combine half of the oil, the peppercorns and garlic; rub over both sides of steaks. *(Make-ahead: Cover and refrigerate for up to 2 hours.)* Sprinkle steaks with salt, patting to adhere.

Grill steaks, covered, on greased grill over medium-high heat, turning once, until desired doneness, about 16 minutes for medium-rare.

Transfer to cutting board; tent with foil and let stand for 5 minutes before slicing. Drizzle with remaining oil.

Store-bought peppercorn medleys usually contain green, black and white peppercorns, which are all seeds from the pepper plant. Both green and black peppercorns are the unripe variety. Green peppercorns are dehydrated quickly to preserve their colour and flavour; black peppercorns are sun-dried, which ferments and darkens them. White peppercorns are picked when they're just about ripe, then sun-dried. Most medleys also contain pink peppercorns, which are the fruit of a different plant.

Makes 4 to 6 servings. PER EACH OF 6 SERVINGS: about 246 cal, 22 g pro, 16 g total fat (4 g sat. fat), 2 g carb, 1 g fibre, 41 mg chol, 445 mg sodium. % RDI: 1% calcium, 24% iron, 2% vit C, 3% folate.

HORSERADISH STRIP LOIN WITH GRILLED PEPPERS

**Strip loin steaks are an inexpensive but tasty option for a simple meal,
but you can substitute any cut of grilling steak that you prefer.**

In small bowl, combine vinegar, mustard and half each of the salt and pepper; gradually drizzle in oil, whisking until emulsified. Stir in horseradish. Set aside 2 tbsp for topping.

Season steaks with remaining salt and pepper. Grill, covered, on greased grill over medium-high heat, brushing often with remaining horseradish mixture and turning once, until medium-rare, about 8 minutes. Transfer to plates and spoon reserved horseradish topping over steaks; let stand for 5 minutes.

Meanwhile, add red peppers and onion to grill; cook, covered, turning occasionally and brushing with remaining horseradish mixture, until softened slightly, about 5 minutes. Serve with steak.

¼ cup **balsamic vinegar**

1 tsp **Dijon mustard**

¼ tsp each **salt** and **coarsely ground pepper**

¼ cup **olive oil**

2 tbsp **prepared horseradish**

2 **beef strip loin grilling steaks** (8 oz/225 g each), halved crosswise

2 **sweet red peppers,** quartered

1 large **Vidalia onion,** cut in ½-inch (1 cm) thick rings

Makes 4 servings. PER SERVING: about 350 cal, 27 g pro, 20 g total fat (4 g sat. fat), 15 g carb, 2 g fibre, 56 mg chol, 242 mg sodium, 510 mg potassium. % RDI: 4% calcium, 22% iron, 22% vit A, 173% vit C, 17% folate.

BEER-BRINED PORK CHOPS

Brining chops in beer gives you juicy, tender and tasty results. For a more intense flavour, use molasses instead of brown sugar. You can mix this dish up by substituting your favourite beer for the dark lager or bock.

2 cups **dark lager** or bock

2 tbsp **coarse salt**

2 tbsp packed **brown sugar**

1 cup **ice cubes**

1 **onion,** sliced

4 **bone-in pork chops** (about 2½ lb/
1.125 kg total), 1 to 1¼ inches
(2.5 to 3 cm) thick

SPICE RUB:

1 tbsp **smoked paprika**

1 tsp each **pepper, garlic powder**
and packed **brown sugar**

½ tsp each **cayenne pepper** and
dried thyme

In baking dish, whisk together beer, salt and brown sugar; stir in ice cubes and onion. Submerge pork in mixture; cover and refrigerate for 12 hours. *(Make-ahead: Refrigerate for up to 24 hours.)*

SPICE RUB: Combine paprika, pepper, garlic powder, brown sugar, cayenne pepper and thyme.

Remove pork from brine; pat dry with paper towel. Rub spice blend over both sides of pork.

Grill pork, covered, on greased grill over medium-high heat, turning once, until juices run clear when pork is pierced and just a hint of pink remains inside, about 8 minutes.

Makes 4 servings. PER SERVING: about 298 cal, 38 g pro, 10 g total fat (3 g sat. fat), 9 g carb, 1 g fibre, 117 mg chol, 446 mg sodium, 604 mg potassium. % RDI: 4% calcium, 14% iron, 9% vit A, 3% vit C, 4% folate.

PAN-FRIED STEAK WITH HORSERADISH RUTABAGA MASH

Rutabaga is an often overlooked (but tasty) root vegetable. With a texture similar to potatoes, rutabaga is delicious mashed or roasted. It is available year-round and stays fresh thanks to its waxy skin. You can use a sharp knife to peel the skin away or buy the vegetable already peeled and cubed.

1 lb (450 g) **beef top sirloin grilling steak**

½ tsp **smoked paprika**

¼ tsp each **salt** and **pepper**

1 tsp **vegetable oil**

HORSERADISH RUTABAGA MASH:

1 **rutabaga** (about 1¾ lb/790 g), peeled and cubed

2 cloves **garlic**

1 lb (450 g) **russet potatoes,** peeled and cubed

¼ cup **light sour cream**

2 tbsp **prepared horseradish**

½ tsp **salt**

¼ tsp **pepper**

¼ cup chopped **fresh chives**

HORSERADISH RUTABAGA MASH: In pot of boiling salted water, cook rutabaga and garlic for 15 minutes; add potatoes. Cook until rutabaga is fork-tender, about 10 minutes; drain.

In food processor, pulse together rutabaga, garlic, potatoes, sour cream, horseradish, salt and pepper until smooth. Stir in chives.

Meanwhile, rub steak all over with paprika, salt and pepper. In cast-iron or nonstick skillet, heat oil over medium-high heat; fry steak, turning once, until medium-rare, 4 to 8 minutes.

Transfer steak to cutting board; let stand, uncovered, for 5 minutes before slicing across the grain. Serve with mash.

Makes 4 servings. PER SERVING: about 307 cal, 28 g pro, 7 g total fat (3 g sat. fat), 34 g carb, 5 g fibre, 55 mg chol, 923 mg sodium, 1,371 mg potassium. % RDI: 12% calcium, 29% iron, 12% vit A, 78% vit C, 20% folate.

SPICY GREENS WITH MAPLE SOY VINAIGRETTE

Slightly spicy mixed bitter greens, such as mizuna, arugula, endive, frisée and watercress, make an ideal backdrop for the vinaigrette's touch of sweetness, but you can use any combination of mixed greens. This salad is refreshing alongside Pan-Fried Steak With Horseradish Mash (opposite)

MAPLE SOY VINAIGRETTE: In large bowl, whisk together vegetable oil, vinegar, soy sauce, maple syrup and sesame oil.

Toss greens and carrot with vinaigrette to coat.

8 cups loosely packed torn **mixed greens**

1 **carrot,** grated

MAPLE SOY VINAIGRETTE:
2 tbsp **vegetable oil**

1 tbsp **unseasoned rice vinegar**

2 tsp **soy sauce**

2 tsp **maple syrup**

1 tsp **sesame oil**

Greens need a thorough washing to remove grit. Place them in a bowl or clean sink filled with cold water. (Running water can bruise delicate leaves.) Swish gently and let grit settle. Lift greens straight up out of the water and into a salad spinner. (Don't pour greens and water into a colander – the grit will resettle into the leaf folds.) Spin for a few seconds, draining between spins. If water still looks gritty, repeat. No salad spinner? Lift greens out of the water and place on a clean tea towel or pillowcase. Gather up the corners and shake gently. Gently wrap large leaves or layer baby greens in a clean tea towel or paper towels and store in the crisper drawer of the fridge.

Makes 4 servings. PER SERVING: about 107 cal, 2 g pro, 8 g total fat (1 g sat. fat), 8 g carb, 2 g fibre, 0 mg chol, 191 mg sodium, 400 mg potassium. % RDI: 7% calcium, 6% iron, 48% vit A, 27% vit C, 44% folate.

MUSTARD SAGE PORK CHOPS WITH ISRAELI COUSCOUS

Tender-crisp edamame add a healthful twist to this wintery pork and mushroom dish. Mustard, chicken broth and sage blend with the pork chop pan juices to create a quick and tasty sauce. Serve with an arugula salad topped with a lemony dressing.

Cook Israeli couscous according to package directions, replacing water with 3 cups of the chicken broth. Meanwhile, cook edamame according to package directions.

Meanwhile, in large nonstick skillet, cook pancetta over medium heat, stirring occasionally, until lightly browned, about 2 minutes. Add garlic and mushrooms; cook until softened, about 4 minutes. Stir into couscous along with edamame and half each of the salt and pepper; keep warm.

In same skillet, melt butter over medium heat. Sprinkle pork with remaining salt and pepper; cook, turning once, until juices run clear when pork is pierced and just a hint of pink remains inside, about 8 minutes.

Transfer couscous mixture to platter; top with pork. Cover and keep warm.

Combine 1 tbsp of the remaining broth with cornstarch; set aside. Add remaining broth to pan; bring to boil over medium-high heat, stirring and scraping up browned bits, until reduced to ½ cup, about 5 minutes.

Whisk in mustard; cook for 1 minute. Stir in sage. Stir in cornstarch mixture; boil until thickened, about 1 minute. Serve over pork and couscous.

1½ cups **Israeli (pearl) couscous**

1 pkg (900 mL) **sodium-reduced chicken broth**

1½ cups **frozen shelled edamame**

⅓ cup diced **pancetta** (about 2½ oz/75 g)

3 cloves **garlic,** minced

12 oz (340 g) **cremini mushrooms,** quartered (about 3½ cups)

¼ tsp each **salt** and **pepper**

1 tbsp **butter**

4 **bone-in pork chops** (about 1¾ lb/ 790 g total)

½ tsp **cornstarch**

4 tsp **Dijon mustard**

1 tbsp chopped **fresh sage**

Makes 4 servings. PER SERVING: about 619 cal, 51 g pro, 21 g total fat (7 g sat. fat), 56 g carb, 6 g fibre, 120 mg chol, 1,120 mg sodium, 1,188 mg potassium. % RDI: 10% calcium, 23% iron, 3% vit A, 5% vit C, 84% folate.

SCALOPPINE WITH TOMATOES

Veal, pork or even turkey cutlets work equally well in this dish packed with the flavours of sun-kissed Italy. It's a simple, elegant main – even for relaxed entertaining.

2 tbsp **extra-virgin olive oil**

1 clove **garlic**

1 can (28 oz/796 mL) **whole tomatoes,** drained and chopped

⅓ cup **dry white wine**

¼ tsp each **salt** and **hot pepper flakes**

8 **veal cutlets,** pork cutlets or turkey cutlets (about 1¼ lb/565 g total)

3 tbsp **all-purpose flour**

1 tbsp **butter**

1 tbsp chopped **fresh parsley**

In large skillet, heat 1 tbsp of the oil over medium-high heat; fry garlic until softened and golden, about 1 minute. Discard garlic.

Add tomatoes, wine, salt and hot pepper flakes; simmer until broken down and no liquid remains, about 10 minutes. Transfer to bowl and keep warm.

Meanwhile, between plastic wrap, pound veal to scant ¼-inch (5 mm) thickness. Place flour in shallow dish; 1 piece at a time, lightly coat veal in flour. Set aside.

In clean skillet, melt butter and remaining oil over medium-high heat; cook veal, in batches, until browned and just a hint of pink remains inside, 4 to 5 minutes. Transfer to serving platter. Pour tomato mixture over top; sprinkle with parsley.

Makes 4 servings. PER SERVING: about 271 cal, 31 g pro, 11 g total fat (3 g sat. fat), 10 g carb, 1 g fibre, 85 mg chol, 433 mg sodium, 816 mg potassium. % RDI: 5% calcium, 19% iron, 5% vit A, 32% vit C, 16% folate.

VEAL CHOPS WITH BLUE CHEESE SAUCE

Wonderfully creamy and decadent, this sauce turns chops into an elegant meal for entertaining. Try whatever blue cheese you prefer – experiment with the best local varieties for the freshest flavour.

Sprinkle veal all over with salt and pepper. In skillet, heat oil over medium-high heat; add butter and garlic. Fry until garlic is lightly browned; with tongs or slotted spoon, remove from skillet. Fry veal, turning once, until golden outside and just pink in centre, 8 to 12 minutes, depending on thickness and desired doneness. Transfer to warmed serving platter; cover and keep warm.

Drain fat from pan; add cider, shallots and vinegar. Bring to boil, stirring and scraping up browned bits from bottom of pan; boil until reduced to about 1 tbsp, 2 to 3 minutes.

Stir in cream; bring to boil. Reduce heat to medium and simmer, stirring, for 2 minutes. Stir in cheese until melted; stir in any accumulated juices from veal. Spoon sauce over veal; sprinkle with chives and parsley.

4 **veal chops** (each 7 to 8 oz/200 to 225 g)
½ tsp **salt**
¼ tsp **pepper**
2 tbsp **olive oil** or vegetable oil
2 tbsp **butter**
2 cloves **garlic,** smashed
¾ cup **apple cider**
¼ cup minced **shallots**
2 tbsp **cider vinegar**
½ cup **whipping cream (35%)**
4 oz (115 g) **Bleu Ermite cheese** or Bleu Bénédictin cheese
2 tbsp finely chopped **fresh chives** and/or **fresh parsley**

Veal chops are so tasty but can be quite pricey. Luckily, this sauce is versatile and is just as luscious over pork chops, which are much more affordable.

Makes 4 servings. PER SERVING: about 494 cal, 31 g pro, 36 g total fat (19 g sat. fat), 11 g carb, trace fibre, 167 mg chol, 824 mg sodium, 593 mg potassium. % RDI: 18% calcium, 11% iron, 20% vit A, 3% vit C, 13% folate.

VEAL CHOPS WITH BLUE CHEESE SAUCE page 107

MUSHROOM SKILLET STEAKS

You can use any fast-fry steak for this simple dish, but boneless rib steaks are tender and flavourful. Serve with egg noodles tossed with a drizzle of olive oil and steamed sugar snap peas.

3 tbsp **extra-virgin olive oil**

2 cloves **garlic,** minced

12 oz (340 g) **cremini mushrooms,** sliced

½ tsp chopped **fresh thyme**

¼ tsp each **salt** and **pepper**

4 thick (½ inch/1 cm) **boneless beef rib grilling steaks** (each 6 oz/170 g)

1 tbsp **all-purpose flour**

½ cup **sodium-reduced beef broth**

In large skillet, heat 2 tbsp of the oil over medium heat; cook garlic until fragrant, about 30 seconds.

Add mushrooms, thyme, salt and pepper; cook, stirring occasionally, until golden, about 8 minutes.

Meanwhile, in separate large skillet, heat remaining oil over medium-high heat; cook steaks, in batches and turning once, until medium-rare, 4 to 6 minutes, or to desired doneness. Transfer to plate; keep warm.

Sprinkle flour into skillet; cook over medium heat, whisking constantly, for 1 minute. Whisk in broth and ½ cup water; bring to boil. Reduce heat to medium-low; simmer until thickened and reduced to ½ cup, about 2 minutes. Spoon sauce and mushrooms over steaks.

Makes 4 servings. PER SERVING: about 460 cal, 39 g pro, 31 g total fat (10 g sat. fat), 6 g carb, 2 g fibre, 89 mg chol, 318 mg sodium, 942 mg potassium. % RDI: 3% calcium, 31% iron, 2% vit C, 9% folate.

GRILLED BACON-STUFFED PORK CHOPS

Get a double dose of pork with these ultraflavourful stuffed chops. For best results, use day-old bread cut into ½-inch (1 cm) cubes. Serve with mixed greens or grilled vegetables.

6 slices **sodium-reduced bacon**

1 small **onion,** finely chopped

2 cloves **garlic,** minced

¼ cup **dry white wine**

2 cups cubed **whole wheat bread**

¼ cup each chopped **fresh basil** and **fresh oregano**

¼ cup grated **Parmesan cheese**

4 **boneless pork chops** (about 1 lb/450 g total)

1 tsp **olive oil**

¼ tsp **pepper**

Pinch **salt**

In large nonstick skillet, cook bacon over medium-high heat until lightly crisp, 5 to 8 minutes. Drain on paper towel–lined plate; coarsely chop.

Drain all but 1 tsp fat from pan; cook onion, stirring often, until softened, about 5 minutes. Add garlic; cook, stirring, until fragrant, about 1 minute.

Add wine; cook, stirring and scraping up browned bits, until reduced by half, about 30 seconds. Turn off heat.

Add bread and ⅓ cup water to pan; cook, stirring, until liquid is absorbed and moist stuffing holds together, adding up to 2 tbsp more water if necessary. Remove from heat. Stir in basil, oregano, Parmesan cheese and bacon. Let cool slightly.

With knife held horizontally and starting at rounded edge of each pork chop, cut pocket almost but not all the way through. Fill each with one-quarter of the stuffing. Brush with oil; sprinkle with pepper and salt.

Grill pork, covered, on greased grill over medium-high heat, turning once, until juices run clear when pork is pierced and just a hint of pink remains inside, 10 to 12 minutes.

Makes 4 servings. PER SERVING: about 288 cal, 34 g pro, 11 g total fat (4 g sat. fat), 11 g carb, 2 g fibre, 71 mg chol, 419 mg sodium, 432 mg potassium. % RDI: 10% calcium, 13% iron, 3% vit A, 3% vit C, 7% folate.

PORK MARSALA

You can substitute any dry white wine you have on hand for the Marsala in this recipe – the chops just won't be as sweet. Tender-crisp green beans and mashed potatoes are perfect fuss-free sides.

Trim pork; sprinkle with half each of the salt and pepper. Place all but 1 tsp of the flour in shallow dish; dredge pork in flour. In large skillet, heat oil over medium-high heat; cook pork, in batches and turning once, until juices run clear when pork is pierced and just a hint of pink remains inside, about 5 minutes. Transfer to plate.

Add shallot and garlic to pan; sauté until softened, about 2 minutes. Add mushrooms, Italian herb seasoning and remaining salt and pepper; sauté, stirring, until golden, about 5 minutes.

Add Marsala; cook until reduced by half. Add broth and ¼ cup water; reduce heat and simmer until reduced by half, about 2 minutes.

Meanwhile, mash butter with remaining flour; stir into sauce and cook until thickened. Return pork to pan; heat through. Sprinkle with parsley.

8 **boneless fast-fry pork loin centre chops** (1 lb/450 g total)

½ tsp each **salt** and **pepper**

2 tbsp **all-purpose flour**

2 tbsp **extra-virgin olive oil**

1 large **shallot** (or half small onion), minced

2 cloves **garlic,** minced

6 oz (170 g) **button mushrooms,** thinly sliced

¼ tsp **dried Italian herb seasoning**

½ cup **sweet Marsala wine** or dry white wine

½ cup **sodium-reduced chicken broth**

1 tsp **butter,** softened

Minced **fresh parsley**

Makes 4 servings. PER SERVING: about 276 cal, 29 g pro, 11 g total fat (3 g sat. fat), 9 g carb, 1 g fibre, 59 mg chol, 421 mg sodium. % RDI: 2% calcium, 11% iron, 1% vit A, 3% vit C, 8% folate.

PORK CHOPS WITH CIDER SAUCE & CREAMY HERB POLENTA

With its sweet cider sauce, this sodium-reduced pork dish is just scrumptious. If you have leftover polenta, form it into cakes and fry them up for a quick side dish to go with your morning eggs.

Rub cut sides of garlic over pork; sprinkle pork with sage and pepper. In large skillet, heat oil over medium-high heat; cook pork, turning once, until juices run clear when pork is pierced and just a hint of pink remains inside, 6 to 8 minutes. Transfer to plate.

Add apple cider and vinegar to pan, scraping up any browned bits. Stir cornstarch with 1 tsp water; whisk into pan juices and cook until thickened, about 1 minute. Return pork to pan and turn to coat.

CREAMY HERB POLENTA: Meanwhile, in saucepan, heat oil over medium-high heat; cook leeks and garlic, stirring occasionally, until softened, about 5 minutes. Add broth, ⅓ cup water, salt and pepper; bring to boil. Reduce heat to medium. Gradually whisk in cornmeal; cook, stirring often, until polenta is thick enough to mound on spoon, 5 to 10 minutes.

Stir in parsley, chives, sour cream, lemon zest, lemon juice and mustard. Serve with pork.

1 clove **garlic,** halved

4 **bone-in pork chops** (about 1⅓ lb/600 g total)

1 tbsp chopped **fresh sage**

½ tsp **pepper**

1 tbsp **olive oil**

1 cup **apple cider**

2 tbsp **cider vinegar**

1 tsp **cornstarch**

CREAMY HERB POLENTA:

1 tbsp **olive oil**

2 **leeks** (white and light green parts), thinly sliced

2 cloves **garlic,** minced

2 cups **no-salt-added chicken broth**

¼ tsp each **salt** and **pepper**

¾ cup **cornmeal**

¼ cup each chopped **fresh parsley** and **fresh chives**

¼ cup **sour cream**

1 tsp grated **lemon zest**

1 tbsp **lemon juice**

2 tsp **Dijon mustard**

Makes 4 servings. PER SERVING: about 415 cal, 27 g pro, 18 g total fat (5 g sat. fat), 38 g carb, 3 g fibre, 79 mg chol, 277 mg sodium, 659 mg potassium. % RDI: 7% calcium, 18% iron, 7% vit A, 18% vit C, 26% folate.

GRILLED VEGETABLES

This generous recipe makes plenty to have on hand as a side to your favourite grilled dishes
(like the yummy pork chops on the opposite page) or as a base for other easy meals.
Try the vegetables tossed with pasta or as a topping for pizza or burgers.

3 each **sweet red peppers** and **sweet yellow peppers**

2 **zucchini**

2 **red onions**

1 **eggplant** (about 1 lb/450 g)

½ tsp **salt**

SEASONED OIL:

⅓ cup **olive oil**

1 clove **garlic,** minced

¼ tsp each **salt** and **pepper**

¼ tsp **hot pepper flakes**

Quarter red and yellow peppers; seed and core. Trim ends off zucchini; cut lengthwise into ¼-inch (5 mm) thick strips. Cut onions into ¼-inch (5 mm) thick rings. Cut eggplant crosswise into ½-inch (1 cm) thick slices.

Place eggplant in colander; sprinkle both sides with salt. Let stand for 30 minutes. Pat dry.

SEASONED OIL: Whisk together oil, garlic, salt, pepper and hot pepper flakes; brush over vegetables.

Grill peppers, covered, on greased grill over medium-high heat, turning once, until grill-marked and tender, 15 to 20 minutes. Remove and let cool enough to handle; coarsely chop.

Repeat with zucchini, grilling for about 8 minutes.

Repeat with onions and eggplant, grilling for about 8 minutes.

Toss together peppers, zucchini, onions and eggplant. *(Make-ahead: Refrigerate in airtight container for up to 3 days.)*

Makes about 12 cups. PER 1 CUP: about 107 cal, 2 g pro, 6 g total fat (1 g sat. fat), 13 g carb, 3 g fibre, 0 mg chol, 99 mg sodium, 298 mg potassium. % RDI: 2% calcium, 4% iron, 15% vit A, 158% vit C, 13% folate.

GRILLED PORK CHOPS WITH PINEAPPLE SALSA

**Spice up your dinner table with a taste of the tropics.
This salsa is also amazing with grilled chicken and fish.**

In shallow dish, whisk together lime juice, soy sauce, ginger, oil and garlic. Add pork, turning to coat. Let stand for 10 minutes.

PINEAPPLE SALSA: Meanwhile, stir together pineapple, green onion, red onion, lime juice, and hot pepper (if using).

Grill pork, covered, on greased grill over medium-high heat, turning once, until juices run clear when pork is pierced and just a hint of pink remains inside, about 8 minutes. Serve with salsa.

3 tbsp each **lime juice** and **soy sauce**

4 tsp grated **fresh ginger**

4 tsp **vegetable oil**

2 cloves **garlic,** minced

4 **bone-in pork chops** (1¾ lb/ 790 g total)

PINEAPPLE SALSA:
Half **pineapple,** peeled, cored and cubed

1 **green onion,** thinly sliced

¼ cup diced **red onion**

2 tsp **lime juice**

1 small **hot pepper** (optional), such as Thai bird's-eye, thinly sliced

TIP

Coring a whole pineapple looks tricky (and a little prickly), but it's pretty straightforward. First, using a sharp chef's knife, cut off the top and bottom, then cut away the skin. Use the tip of a potato peeler to poke out the brown "eyes." Then cut the pineapple lengthwise into quarters to expose the core. Slice off the core from each quarter and you're done!

Makes 4 servings. PER SERVING: about 277 cal, 28 g pro, 13 g total fat (4 g sat. fat), 11 g carb, 1 g fibre, 77 mg chol, 694 mg sodium, 497 mg potassium. % RDI: 4% calcium, 11% iron, 1% vit A, 42% vit C, 9% folate.

ORANGE-GLAZED PORK CHOPS WITH HAZELNUT GREEN BEANS

**To make the tastiest sauce, use freshly squeezed orange juice.
On another night, try this recipe with grilled chicken breasts or thighs instead of the pork.**

4 **bone-in pork chops** (about 1¾ lb/
    790 g total)
Pinch each **salt** and **pepper**
2 tsp **vegetable oil**
2 cloves **garlic,** minced
2 tsp grated **fresh ginger**
1 cup **sodium-reduced chicken broth**
½ cup **orange juice**

HAZELNUT GREEN BEANS:
1 lb (450 g) **green beans,** trimmed
1 tbsp **olive oil**
2 tsp **lemon juice**
1 clove **garlic,** minced
Pinch each **salt** and **pepper**
⅓ cup chopped toasted **hazelnuts**

Sprinkle pork with salt and pepper. In large nonstick skillet, heat half of the oil over medium heat; cook pork until juices run clear when pork is pierced and just a hint of pink remains inside, 8 to 12 minutes. Transfer to plate.

Drain any fat from pan; heat remaining oil over medium heat. Cook garlic and ginger until fragrant, about 2 minutes. Stir in broth and orange juice; bring to boil. Boil, stirring often, until thick enough to coat spoon, about 6 minutes. Return pork and any accumulated juices to pan; cook, turning once, until glazed, about 2 minutes.

HAZELNUT GREEN BEANS: Meanwhile, in large pot of boiling salted water, cook green beans until tender-crisp, 2 to 3 minutes; drain. In large bowl, toss together beans, oil, lemon juice, garlic, salt and pepper; sprinkle with hazelnuts. Serve with pork.

Makes 4 servings. PER SERVING: about 358 cal, 31 g pro, 21 g total fat (4 g sat. fat), 14 g carb, 3 g fibre, 77 mg chol, 430 mg sodium, 628 mg potassium. % RDI: 8% calcium, 16% iron, 7% vit A, 38% vit C, 25% folate.

PORK SALTIMBOCCA

In Italian, *saltimbocca* means "to jump in the mouth" – or so tasty you can't stop eating it! Saltimbocca most often features veal, but this scrumptious pork version is just as good.

1½ lb (675 g) **boneless pork loin**

½ tsp **pepper**

8 slices **prosciutto**

8 large **fresh sage leaves**

2 tbsp **all-purpose flour**

2 tbsp **extra-virgin olive oil**

⅔ cup **sodium-reduced chicken broth**

⅓ cup **sweet Marsala wine**

1 tbsp finely chopped **fresh chives** or parsley

Cut pork into 8 pieces. Between plastic wrap and using flat side of meat mallet, pound each piece to ¼-inch (5 mm) thickness. Sprinkle each with pepper; top each with 1 slice prosciutto.

For each piece, place 1 sage leaf on prosciutto at short end; starting at short end, roll up. Secure with wooden pick. Place in bowl. *(Make-ahead: Cover and refrigerate for up to 12 hours.)*

Sprinkle rolls with flour, tossing to coat. In large skillet, heat oil over medium-high heat; shaking off excess flour, sear rolls on all sides until golden, about 3 minutes. Transfer to plate.

Drain fat from pan. Pour in broth and Marsala; bring to boil, stirring and scraping up browned bits. Return rolls to pan, cover and simmer until juices run clear when pork is pierced and just a hint of pink remains inside, about 3 minutes. Transfer to platter; remove picks.

Boil pan juices until reduced to ⅓ cup, about 3 minutes. Strain over rolls; sprinkle with chives.

Makes 4 servings. PER SERVING: about 337 cal, 45 g pro, 12 g total fat (3 g sat. fat), 7 g carb, trace fibre, 119 mg chol, 575 mg sodium. % RDI: 5% calcium, 14% iron, 1% vit A, 3% vit C, 7% folate.

SWEET & SMOKY PORK CHOP DINNER

This easy dish for two lets all the ingredients mingle on one baking sheet for rich flavour. Roasting the pork on top of the vegetables allows heat to surround the chops, helping them cook faster.

Stir together brown sugar, paprika, onion powder, mustard powder and pinch of the garlic powder; rub all over pork. Set aside.

Sprinkle bacon over half of foil-lined baking sheet. Sprinkle potato with salt, pepper and remaining garlic powder; place on bacon. Roast in 425°F (220°C) oven for 20 minutes. Turn potato wedges.

Meanwhile, stir together grainy mustard, maple syrup and vinegar; toss with brussels sprouts and apple. Spread over empty side of baking sheet. Roast until brussels sprouts are tender and browned, 25 minutes.

Place pork on brussels sprouts mixture; roast until juices run clear when pork is pierced and just a hint of pink remains inside, and potatoes are tender and browned, 8 to 10 minutes.

1 tsp packed **brown sugar**

½ tsp **smoked paprika**

¼ tsp each **onion powder** and **mustard powder**

¼ tsp **garlic powder**

2 **bone-in pork chops** (about 12 oz/340 g total), ½ inch (1 cm) thick

2 slices **bacon,** cut in ½-inch (1 cm) pieces

1 large **russet potato,** cut in ½-inch (1 cm) thick wedges

Pinch each **salt** and **pepper**

2 tsp **grainy mustard**

1 tsp **maple syrup**

1 tsp **balsamic vinegar**

1 lb (450 g) **brussels sprouts,** trimmed and halved

1 **apple,** cut in 1-inch (2.5 cm) chunks

TIP When you're trimming fresh brussels sprouts, peel off any wilted outer leaves. Using a sharp paring knife, cut sprouts in half lengthwise. Trim off any brown oxidized bits of the core but keep the core intact to hold the leaves together as the sprouts are cooking.

Makes 2 servings. PER SERVING: about 577 cal, 39 g pro, 20 g total fat (8 g sat. fat), 65 g carb, 12 g fibre, 98 mg chol, 333 mg sodium, 1,987 mg potassium. % RDI: 13% calcium, 39% iron, 21% vit A, 280% vit C, 73% folate.

STEAK & BROWN RICE BURRITO BOWL

Trade in your regular steak burrito for this health-smart version, which is loaded with kale, red pepper and black beans. Using whole grain parboiled brown rice pares down the cooking time, so you can whip up this dish in a hurry. Top with salsa, fresh cilantro or sliced green onions.

BLACK BEANS & RICE: In large saucepan, heat oil over medium-high heat; cook garlic, chili powder, coriander and cumin, stirring, until fragrant, about 1 minute. Stir in 1¼ cups water, rice, beans, strained tomatoes, salt and pepper. Bring to boil; cover and cook until rice is tender, about 20 minutes. Remove from heat; let stand, covered, until liquid is absorbed, about 5 minutes.

Meanwhile, stir together coriander, cumin and half each of the salt and pepper; rub all over steaks.

In large nonstick skillet, heat half of the oil over medium-high heat; cook steaks, turning once, until medium-rare, 6 to 8 minutes. Transfer to plate; let stand for 5 minutes before thinly slicing.

Meanwhile, in same skillet, heat remaining oil over medium heat; cook onion and chili powder until softened, about 3 minutes. Stir in kale, red pepper, 3 tbsp water, and remaining salt and pepper; cook, stirring often, until kale is wilted and pepper is tender-crisp, about 6 minutes.

Divide rice mixture among bowls; top with kale mixture and steak.

¼ tsp each **ground coriander** and **ground cumin**

¼ tsp each **salt** and **pepper**

2 **beef tenderloin grilling steaks** (12 oz/340 g total)

2 tsp **olive oil**

1 small **onion,** sliced

½ tsp **chili powder**

3 cups thinly sliced stemmed **kale** (about half bunch)

1 **sweet red pepper,** sliced

BLACK BEANS & RICE:

1 tsp **olive oil**

2 cloves **garlic,** minced

1 tsp each **chili powder, ground coriander** and **ground cumin**

¾ cup **whole grain parboiled brown rice** (such as Uncle Ben's)

¾ cup rinsed drained **canned black beans**

½ cup **bottled strained tomatoes** (passata)

¼ tsp each **salt** and **pepper**

Makes 4 servings. PER SERVING: about 386 cal, 26 g pro, 11 g total fat (4 g sat. fat), 46 g carb, 6 g fibre, 47 mg chol, 565 mg sodium, 915 mg potassium. % RDI: 11% calcium, 41% iron, 83% vit A, 172% vit C, 22% folate.

SPICED PORK CHOPS WITH PEAR RELISH

Switch up the classic pork-and-applesauce combination with this spicy-sweet pear relish that whips up in just 25 minutes.

2 tsp each **ground cumin** and **ground coriander**

¼ tsp each **salt** and **pepper**

4 **bone-in pork loin centre chops** (about 2 lb/900 g total)

2 tsp **vegetable oil**

PEAR RELISH:

2 tsp **vegetable oil**

1 small **onion,** sliced

2 slices (¼ inch/5 mm thick) **fresh ginger**

1 stick **cinnamon**

2 **whole cloves**

1 **pear,** peeled, quartered and sliced crosswise

¼ cup **golden raisins**

2 tbsp **cider vinegar**

2 tsp packed **brown sugar**

PEAR RELISH: In saucepan, heat oil over medium heat; cook onion, ginger, cinnamon and cloves, stirring occasionally, until onion is softened, about 5 minutes.

Stir in pear, raisins, ¼ cup water, vinegar and brown sugar; bring to boil. Reduce heat and simmer, stirring occasionally, until pear is softened, about 15 minutes.

Meanwhile, stir together cumin, coriander, salt and pepper; rub all over pork. In large skillet, heat oil over medium heat; cook pork, turning once, until juices run clear when pork is pierced and just a hint of pink remains inside, 10 to 12 minutes. Serve with relish.

Makes 4 servings. PER SERVING: about 327 cal, 31 g pro, 15 g total fat (4 g sat. fat), 17 g carb, 2 g fibre, 87 mg chol, 221 mg sodium, 573 mg potassium. % RDI: 5% calcium, 16% iron, 1% vit A, 5% vit C, 3% folate.

SWISS CHARD WITH MUSHROOMS

**Earthy mushrooms and Swiss chard are wonderful partners in recipes.
Keep this simple side in your recipe box to make the most of an ample greens harvest in the summer.**

Remove stems from Swiss chard. Thinly slice stems and shred leaves; place in separate bowls. Seed, core and thinly slice red pepper.

In large shallow Dutch oven, heat oil over medium-high heat; sauté mushrooms, garlic, salt, Swiss chard stems and red pepper until no liquid remains, about 7 minutes.

Add Swiss chard leaves; cover and cook until wilted, about 3 minutes.

2 bunches **Swiss chard** (about 2 lb/900 g total)

1 **sweet red pepper**

2 tbsp **extra-virgin olive oil**

1½ cups coarsely chopped **mushrooms**

2 cloves **garlic,** minced

¾ tsp **salt**

Swiss chard stems and leaves are both edible – and totally delicious – but they cook at different rates. The stems need a bit longer than the delicate leaves to get tender, so make sure to separate them and add the stems first.

Makes 4 to 6 servings. PER EACH OF 6 SERVINGS: about 75 cal, 3 g pro, 5 g total fat (1 g sat. fat), 7 g carb, 3 g fibre, 0 mg chol, 514 mg sodium. % RDI: 7% calcium, 23% iron, 47% vit A, 93% vit C, 7% folate.

ROSEMARY-DIJON GRILLED LAMB CHOPS & SMASHED POTATOES

Grilling chops is quicker and easier than manoeuvring an entire rack of lamb on the barbecue. Stirring reserved potato cooking liquid and olive oil into the smashed potatoes gives them a creamy texture without adding any cream or butter.

2 lb (900 g) **potatoes,** peeled and quartered

6 cloves **garlic**

3 tbsp **extra-virgin olive oil**

1 tsp **pepper**

¾ tsp **salt**

¼ cup chopped **fresh chives**

2 tbsp finely chopped **fresh rosemary**

1 tbsp **Dijon mustard**

8 **lamb loin chops** (about 1¼ lb/ 565 g total)

In saucepan of boiling lightly salted water, cook potatoes and 4 of the garlic cloves until potatoes are tender, about 15 minutes.

Reserving ½ cup of the cooking liquid, drain; transfer potatoes and garlic to large bowl. Add reserved cooking liquid, oil and half each of the pepper and salt; smash with potato masher until smooth with a few chunks remaining. Stir in chives. Keep warm.

Mince remaining garlic. Combine garlic, rosemary, mustard, and remaining pepper and salt. Rub all over lamb. Grill, covered, on greased grill over medium-high heat, turning once, until desired doneness, about 8 minutes for medium-rare. Serve with potatoes.

Makes 4 servings. PER SERVING: about 366 cal, 18 g pro, 16 g total fat (4 g sat. fat), 39 g carb, 3 g fibre, 32 mg chol, 1,014 mg sodium, 805 mg potassium. % RDI: 4% calcium, 14% iron, 2% vit A, 27% vit C, 13% folate.

MOROCCAN-SPICED PORK TENDERLOIN WITH CARROT SALAD

Slicing a pork tenderloin into medallions reduces the cooking time significantly compared with roasting it whole. Serve this fragrant spiced dish with roasted baby potatoes or couscous.

4 cups shredded **carrots** (4 large)

2 **green onions,** thinly sliced

¼ cup **olive oil**

¼ cup **lemon juice**

2 tbsp chopped **fresh cilantro**

2 tbsp **liquid honey**

1 tsp **ground cumin**

½ tsp **salt**

1 lb (450 g) **pork tenderloin,** trimmed

½ tsp **sweet paprika**

¼ tsp each **cinnamon** and **pepper**

In large bowl, combine carrots, green onions, 2 tbsp of the oil, 3 tbsp of the lemon juice, the cilantro, 1 tbsp of the honey, ½ tsp of the cumin and ¼ tsp of the salt.

Cut pork into eight 1-inch (2.5 cm) thick medallions.

Reserve 1 tbsp of the remaining oil. In bowl, combine paprika, cinnamon, pepper and remaining oil, lemon juice, honey, cumin and salt; sprinkle over pork, gently rubbing into meat.

In cast-iron or heavy skillet, heat reserved oil over medium heat; cook pork, turning occasionally, until juices run clear when pork is pierced and just a hint of pink remains inside, 3 to 4 minutes. Serve with carrot salad.

Makes 4 servings. PER SERVING: about 332 cal, 26 g pro, 16 g total fat (3 g sat. fat), 21 g carb, 3 g fibre, 61 mg chol, 420 mg sodium, 769 mg potassium. % RDI: 5% calcium, 16% iron, 135% vit A, 20% vit C, 15% folate.

PEPPERED LAMB CHOPS WITH MINT BUTTER

Mint and lamb are a classic pairing for good reason. But if you can't get fresh mint, parsley is yummy too.
As an alternative to chops, **try New Zealand lamb medallions, which are available frozen in packages of four.**

MINT BUTTER: Mash together butter, mint, vinegar, shallot and pepper. On plastic wrap, shape into 3-inch (8 cm) long log; wrap and seal ends. Refrigerate until firm, 30 minutes. *(Make-ahead: Overwrap in foil; freeze for up to 2 weeks.)*

Rub lamb with oil; sprinkle with pepper. Grill, covered, on greased grill over medium-high heat, turning once, until desired doneness, about 8 to 10 minutes for medium-rare.

Transfer lamb to platter. Cut mint butter into 8 slices; top each chop with 1 butter slice.

8 **lamb loin chops** or rib chops, frenched
2 tsp **vegetable oil**
1 tbsp coarsely ground **pepper**

MINT BUTTER:
¼ cup **butter,** softened
1 tbsp chopped **fresh mint**
2 tsp **white wine vinegar**
1 **shallot,** minced
½ tsp **pepper**

Frenching lamb chops is quite simple and gives them a polished restaurant look. Using a sharp carving knife, scrape clean the ends of each rib bone to within 1 inch (2.5 cm) of the eye of the raw meat. That's it!

Makes 4 servings. PER SERVING: about 241 cal, 17 g pro, 19 g total fat (10 g sat. fat), 2 g carb, 1 g fibre, 69 mg chol, 145 mg sodium, 236 mg potassium. % RDI: 2% calcium, 13% iron, 11% vit A, 2% vit C, 5% folate.

BLACK BEAN BEEF & VEGETABLE STIR-FRY

Different brands of black bean sauce can vary in flavour and saltiness. Try a few different ones to discover your favourite. If flank steak is unavailable, use any beef grilling steak or pork.

Sprinkle beef with pepper. Whisk together broth, black bean sauce and cornstarch. Set aside.

In wok or skillet, heat half of the oil over medium-high heat; stir-fry beef until browned but still pink inside, about 3 minutes. Transfer to plate.

Add remaining oil to wok; stir-fry garlic and ginger for 30 seconds. Add broccoli, orange peppers and onion; stir-fry for 2 minutes. Cover and steam for 2 minutes.

Return beef and any accumulated juices to wok. Add black bean mixture; stir-fry until slightly thickened, about 3 minutes. Drizzle with sesame oil.

12 oz (340 g) **beef flank marinating steak,** thinly sliced across the grain

½ tsp **pepper**

1 cup **sodium-reduced beef broth**

3 tbsp **black bean sauce**

1 tbsp **cornstarch**

2 tbsp **vegetable oil**

2 cloves **garlic,** minced

1 tbsp minced **fresh ginger**

2 cups **broccoli florets**

2 **sweet orange peppers** or sweet red peppers, cut in chunks

1 **white onion,** cut in chunks

1 tsp **sesame oil**

Makes 4 servings. PER SERVING: about 307 cal, 22 g pro, 16 g total fat (4 g sat. fat), 20 g carb, 2 g fibre, 40 mg chol, 409 mg sodium, 739 mg potassium. % RDI: 5% calcium, 18% iron, 21% vit A, 193% vit C, 20% folate.

STEAK & PEPPER STIR-FRY

This stir-fry comes together in minutes, with a lot less chopping than you'd expect. Serve with steamed rice or noodles to soak up the sauce. For a spicy kick, add 1 tsp (or more) chili garlic paste.

2 tbsp **oyster sauce**

1 tsp **cornstarch**

Pinch each **salt** and **pepper**

1 tbsp **vegetable oil**

1 lb (450 g) **beef flank marinating steak,** thinly sliced across the grain

1 **onion,** sliced

2 **sweet peppers** (red, orange and/or yellow), sliced

Combine 3 tbsp water, oyster sauce, cornstarch, salt and pepper. Set aside.

In large nonstick skillet or wok, heat 2 tsp of the oil over high heat; stir-fry beef until browned, about 3 minutes. Transfer to plate.

Add remaining oil, onion and 2 tbsp water to pan. Stir-fry over medium-high heat, scraping up browned bits, until softened, about 4 minutes. Add peppers; stir-fry until tender-crisp, about 4 minutes.

Return beef to skillet. Add oyster sauce mixture; cook, tossing to coat, until sauce is slightly thickened, about 1 minute.

Makes 4 servings. PER SERVING: about 249 cal, 26 g pro, 13 g total fat (4 g sat. fat), 8 g carb, 1 g fibre, 53 mg chol, 316 mg sodium, 521 mg potassium. % RDI: 2% calcium, 17% iron, 11% vit A, 157% vit C, 9% folate.

PORK, ZUCCHINI & ALMOND STIR-FRY

**Need a weeknight dinner with interesting flavours and a delightfully crunchy texture?
This stir-fry fills the bill with healthful almonds and lean pork tenderloin.**

Toss together pork, vinegar, fennel seeds, ½ tsp of the salt, the hot pepper flakes and pepper.

In wok, heat half of the oil over high heat; stir-fry pork mixture until lightly browned and just slightly pink inside, 2 to 3 minutes. Transfer to plate. Wipe out wok.

Heat remaining oil in wok over medium heat; fry zucchini, garlic, almonds, oregano and remaining salt until zucchini is lightly browned and tender-crisp, 3 to 4 minutes. Add parsley and pork with any accumulated juices; stir-fry until pork is hot, about 1 minute.

TIP If you have a nonstick wok, high heat can damage the finish and ruin the pan. Either turn down the heat to medium-high (maximum) or use an uncoated steel wok to stir up this dish.

---

12 oz (340 g) **pork tenderloin** or pork loin, cut in ¾-inch (2 cm) chunks

2 tsp **balsamic vinegar**

1 tsp **fennel seeds**

¾ tsp **salt**

¼ tsp **hot pepper flakes**

Pinch **pepper**

2 tbsp **extra-virgin olive oil**

2 small **green zucchini** or yellow zucchini, cut in ¾-inch (2 cm) chunks

2 cloves **garlic,** thinly sliced

½ cup **natural almonds**

½ tsp **dried oregano**

¼ cup chopped **fresh parsley**

Makes 4 servings. PER SERVING: about 271 cal, 23 g pro, 17 g total fat (2 g sat. fat), 7 g carb, 3 g fibre, 47 mg chol, 482 mg sodium, 621 mg potassium. % RDI: 7% calcium, 18% iron, 9% vit A, 13% vit C, 10% folate.

OVEN-BAKED RIBS WITH MAPLE BARBECUE SAUCE

Sticky, spicy and sweet, these ribs roast up comparatively quickly in the oven, saving you lots of hands-on cooking time. The maple barbecue sauce is great on chicken too.

3 lb (1.35 kg) **pork back ribs** or
   side ribs

½ tsp **salt**

1 tbsp **sweet paprika**

1 tbsp **granulated sugar**

1 tsp **ground cumin**

½ tsp **ground coriander**

½ tsp **cayenne pepper**

½ tsp **dried oregano**

MAPLE BARBECUE SAUCE:

½ cup **ketchup**

2 tbsp **cider vinegar**

1 tbsp **maple syrup**

1 tbsp **Worcestershire sauce**

1 tsp **chili powder**

Sprinkle ribs all over with salt. Combine paprika, sugar, cumin, coriander, cayenne and oregano; rub all over ribs. Place on rack in roasting pan; roast in 425°F (220°C) oven for 45 minutes, turning once. Pour off fat.

MAPLE BARBECUE SAUCE: Meanwhile, in saucepan, bring ketchup, vinegar, maple syrup, Worcestershire sauce and chili powder to boil. Reduce heat and simmer, stirring often, for 10 minutes. Brush all over ribs. Roast until sticky, about 10 minutes.

Makes 4 servings. PER SERVING: about 568 cal, 40 g pro, 38 g total fat (15 g sat. fat), 17 g carb, 2 g fibre, 154 mg chol, 567 mg sodium, 696 mg potassium. % RDI: 8% calcium, 22% iron, 14% vit A, 12% vit C, 5% folate.

STOUT-GLAZED BEEF RIBS

Beer and ribs are such an ideal match that everyone will ask for more. Pork ribs make a nice alternative – just cut them into two-rib portions and add one hour to the braising time.

4½ lb (2.025 kg) **beef back ribs,** cut in 1-rib portions

½ tsp each **salt** and **pepper**

2 bottles (each 341 mL) **stout**

1 **onion,** sliced

3 cloves **garlic,** sliced

½ cup packed **brown sugar**

¼ cup **tomato paste**

3 tbsp drained **prepared horseradish**

2 tbsp **Dijon mustard**

1 tbsp **Worcestershire sauce**

Rub meaty side of ribs with salt and pepper; place, meaty side down, in roasting pan. Add stout, onion and garlic; cover and braise in 325°F (160°C) oven until fork-tender, about 1¼ hours.

Transfer ribs to plate. Skim fat from braising liquid; strain, discarding onion. Pour 1½ cups braising liquid into saucepan; whisk in brown sugar, tomato paste, horseradish, mustard and Worcestershire sauce. Bring to boil over medium-high heat, whisking frequently; cook until thickened and reduced to 1 cup, about 15 minutes.

Grill ribs, covered, on greased grill over medium-high heat, basting with sauce every few minutes, until caramelized, 12 to 15 minutes.

Makes 4 servings. PER SERVING: about 484 cal, 31 g pro, 22 g total fat (10 g sat. fat), 38 g carb, 1 g fibre, 75 mg chol, 473 mg sodium, 728 mg potassium. % RDI: 7% calcium, 27% iron, 2% vit A, 12% vit C, 11% folate.

FIVE SPICE-RUBBED PORK RIBS

Five-spice powder, which usually combines cinnamon, anise, fennel, Szechuan pepper and cloves, is the perfect base for this spice rub. The slow and even cooking of indirect heat creates the most tender ribs without burning the meat.

FIVE-SPICE RUB: Combine five-spice powder, coriander, brown sugar, garlic powder and pepper.

Remove membrane (if attached) from underside of ribs. Rub spice mixture onto ribs, massaging into meat. Cover and refrigerate for 1 hour. *(Make-ahead: Refrigerate for up to 24 hours.)*

Heat 1 burner of 2-burner barbecue, or 2 outside burners of 3-burner barbecue, to medium. Place ribs, meaty side up, on greased grill over unlit burner. Grill, covered, until fork-tender, about 1½ hours.

In saucepan, heat oil over medium heat; cook green onions, garlic and ginger until fragrant, about 1 minute. Add orange juice, hoisin sauce, vinegar and salt; bring to boil. Reduce heat and simmer until glaze is thickened slightly, about 3 minutes.

Transfer ribs to direct heat; brush with glaze. Grill, uncovered, turning occasionally and brushing with glaze, until slightly sticky, about 10 minutes.

2 racks **pork back ribs** (about 3½ lb/1.5 kg total)

1 tsp **vegetable oil**

3 **green onions,** thinly sliced

3 cloves **garlic,** minced

2 tsp grated **fresh ginger**

⅓ cup **orange juice**

¼ cup **hoisin sauce**

1 tbsp **unseasoned rice vinegar**

Pinch **salt**

FIVE-SPICE RUB:
1 tbsp **five-spice powder**

2 tsp **ground coriander**

2 tsp packed **brown sugar**

1 tsp **garlic powder**

1 tsp **pepper**

Makes 4 to 6 servings. PER EACH OF 6 SERVINGS: about 443 cal, 31 g pro, 30 g total fat (11 g sat. fat), 11 g carb, 1 g fibre, 120 mg chol, 317 mg sodium, 458 mg potassium. % RDI: 7% calcium, 15% iron, 1% vit A, 12% vit C, 6% folate.

LAMB CHOPS WITH SPINACH BIRYANI

Vibrantly spiced biryani, earthy spinach and delicate lamb make a party dish to remember. You can make the biryani as spicy as you like by choosing the heat level of your curry paste. If it's too cold to barbecue, just broil the chops until medium-rare.

½ tsp **salt**

¼ tsp each **ground cumin** and **ground coriander**

8 **lamb loin chops**

SPINACH BIRYANI:

1 tbsp **vegetable oil**

1 **onion,** diced

2 cloves **garlic,** minced

1 tbsp **curry paste**

¼ tsp each **salt** and **pepper**

1 cup **basmati rice**

¼ cup **raisins**

1 cup **sodium-reduced chicken broth**

4 cups chopped **fresh spinach**

¼ cup toasted **sliced almonds**

SPINACH BIRYANI: In large saucepan, heat oil over medium heat; cook onion until deep golden, about 8 minutes. Add garlic, curry paste, salt and pepper; cook, stirring, until fragrant, about 2 minutes. Stir in rice and raisins to coat.

Add broth and 1 cup water; bring to boil. Reduce heat, cover and simmer until almost no liquid remains, about 20 minutes. Stir in spinach and almonds. Cover and let stand for 5 minutes.

Meanwhile, combine salt, cumin and coriander; rub over lamb. Grill, covered, on greased grill over medium-high heat, turning once, until medium-rare, 8 to 12 minutes. Serve with biryani.

Makes 4 servings. PER SERVING: about 504 cal, 35 g pro, 18 g total fat (4 g sat. fat), 50 g carb, 3 g fibre, 87 mg chol, 786 mg sodium, 688 mg potassium. % RDI: 9% calcium, 27% iron, 30% vit A, 7% vit C, 34% folate.

LAMB LOIN CHOPS WITH PIMIENTO OLIVE BUTTER

Chops are quick to cook. If you make the butter and rub the lamb in the morning, you'll have dinner on the table just 15 minutes after you get home.

PIMIENTO OLIVE BUTTER: Stir together butter, olives, mustard and oregano until smooth. Spoon onto plastic wrap; shape into log and tightly wrap. Refrigerate until firm, about 1 hour. Slice into ¼-inch (5 mm) thick rounds.

Meanwhile, mix together oil, rosemary, thyme, oregano, fennel seeds, garlic and pepper; rub all over lamb. Cover and refrigerate for 1 hour. *(Make-ahead: Refrigerate butter and lamb separately for up to 24 hours.)*

Grill lamb, covered, on greased grill over medium-high heat, turning once, until desired doneness, about 10 minutes for medium-rare. Serve with pimiento olive butter.

2 tbsp **extra-virgin olive oil**

1 tbsp minced **fresh rosemary**

1 tsp each **dried thyme** and **dried oregano**

1 tsp **fennel seeds,** crushed

1 clove **garlic,** minced

½ tsp **pepper**

8 **lamb loin chops**

PIMIENTO OLIVE BUTTER:

2 tbsp **butter,** softened

2 tsp finely diced **pimiento-stuffed olives**

¼ tsp **Dijon mustard**

Pinch **dried oregano**

TIP

This flavoured butter is good on just about everything. Make a double batch, wrap the extras tightly in plastic wrap and freeze in a resealable freezer bag for up to a month. Enjoy it on grilled steaks, vegetables, poultry and fish.

Makes 4 servings. PER SERVING: about 238 cal, 18 g pro, 18 g total fat (7 g sat. fat), 1 g carb, 1 g fibre, 84 mg chol, 101 mg sodium. % RDI: 3% calcium, 15% iron, 6% vit A, 2% vit C, 1% folate.

OVEN ROASTS

RECIPES

PORCINI-DUSTED BEEF TENDERLOIN WITH ONION JUS

**Beef tenderloin is an occasion in and of itself.
Porcinis and Port make it even more sumptuous – perfect for a splashy entertaining meal.**

1 pkg (14 g) **dried porcini mushrooms**

½ tsp each **salt** and **pepper**

2 lb (900 g) **beef tenderloin premium oven roast,** tied at 1½-inch (4 cm) intervals

1 tbsp each **vegetable oil** and **butter**

12 **shallots**

2 cups halved small **white mushrooms** (about 6 oz/170 g)

1 cup **Port** or sodium-reduced chicken broth

1 cup **sodium-reduced chicken broth**

2 tbsp **balsamic vinegar**

1 tbsp **Dijon mustard**

BEURRE MANIÉ:

1½ tsp **butter,** softened

1½ tsp **all-purpose flour**

BEURRE MANIÉ: Mash butter with flour until smooth; refrigerate for 15 minutes. (*Make-ahead: Refrigerate for up to 24 hours.*)

Meanwhile, in spice grinder or using mortar and pestle, grind porcini mushrooms until fine powder. In large shallow dish, stir together porcinis and all but pinch each of the salt and pepper. Rub all over roast.

In large skillet, heat half each of the oil and butter over medium-high heat; brown roast all over. Transfer to rack in roasting pan. Roast in 425°F (220°C) oven until instant-read thermometer inserted in centre reads 140°F (60°C) for medium-rare, about 35 minutes.

Transfer roast to cutting board; tent with foil. Let stand for 10 minutes before carving into ½-inch (1 cm) thick slices.

Meanwhile, peel and halve shallots lengthwise, keeping root end intact. Heat remaining oil and butter in same skillet over medium-high heat; sauté shallots, white mushrooms and remaining salt and pepper until golden, about 5 minutes.

Add Port, broth, vinegar and mustard; bring to boil. Reduce heat and simmer until shallots are tender, 15 to 17 minutes. Whisk in beurre manié until smooth and thickened. (*Make-ahead: Let cool. Refrigerate in airtight container for up to 2 days.*) Serve sauce with beef.

Beurre manié (French for "kneaded butter") is a simple thickener for soups, stews and gravies. It's a mix of equal parts flour and butter, mashed together until smooth. You can stir it straight into a sauce or gravy and it thickens beautifully with no lumps.

Makes 6 to 8 servings. PER EACH OF 8 SERVINGS: about 239 cal, 25 g pro, 9 g total fat (4 g sat. fat), 9 g carb, 1 g fibre, 59 mg chol, 315 mg sodium. % RDI: 2% calcium, 24% iron, 3% vit A, 2% vit C, 6% folate.

ROTISSERIE PRIME RIB

Rotisserie roasts come prepped and ready for the barbecue – they're ideal for cooking on a spit or over indirect heat. Prime rib is meltingly tender, so it doesn't take much seasoning to make it a pleasure to eat.

4 cloves **garlic,** minced

1½ tsp **salt**

½ tsp **pepper**

1 tbsp **olive oil**

4 lb (1.8 kg) **boneless beef prime rib premium rotisserie roast**

7 sprigs **fresh rosemary**

On cutting board, smash garlic with side of chef's knife; rub in salt and pepper to make paste. Mix with oil; rub over roast. Slip rosemary under strings all around roast. Clamp 1 end of roast with rotisserie fork; insert spit and clamp into other end.

Follow manufacturer's instructions for using rotisserie. Or, for 3-burner barbecue, remove grill racks. Place foil drip pan along centre of barbecue. Pour water into pan to depth of 1 inch (2.5 cm). Heat barbecue to medium-high. Turn centre burner off. Place roast on barbecue, centring over drip pan. Start rotisserie.

Reduce heat to medium; grill, covered, until instant-read thermometer inserted in centre reads 140°F (60°C) for medium-rare, about 70 minutes.

Transfer roast to cutting board; pull out forks and spit. Tent with foil; let stand for 20 minutes before carving.

Makes 8 servings. PER SERVING: about 339 cal, 43 g pro, 16 g total fat (7 g sat. fat), 1 g carb, trace fibre, 93 mg chol, 530 mg sodium. % RDI: 2% calcium, 24% iron, 4% folate.

ROAST BEEF WITH MUSHROOM GRAVY

Oven roast cuts of beef – such as sirloin tip, and inside and outside round – are less expensive than premium cuts and can make fine roasts. However, because they are less marbled with fat, they need help to keep them succulent. A tasty garlic-and-herb-infused butter is just the ticket.

½ cup **butter,** softened

3 cloves **garlic,** pressed

4 tsp minced **fresh thyme**
(or 1½ tsp dried)

½ tsp **anchovy paste** (optional)

¼ tsp **white pepper**

Pinch **ground cloves**

2 tbsp **all-purpose flour**

4 lb (1.8 kg) **beef sirloin tip oven roast,** or beef inside or outside round oven roast

1¼ tsp **salt**

½ tsp **pepper**

1 **onion,** thinly sliced

2 tbsp **brandy** or whisky (optional)

1 cup **sodium-reduced beef broth**

¼ cup **dry sherry,** white wine or dry white vermouth (or 1 tbsp lemon juice)

12 oz (340 g) **mushrooms,** sliced

¼ cup finely chopped **fresh parsley**

2 tsp **Dijon mustard**

Using fork, mash together butter, garlic, thyme, anchovy paste (if using), white pepper and cloves. Transfer 2 tbsp to small bowl; mash with flour. Set aside.

With long thin knife, make 12 evenly spaced cuts halfway to bottom of roast. Enlarge each hole with handle of wooden spoon; stuff about 1 tsp of the flourless butter mixture into each. Sprinkle roast with 1 tsp of the salt and the pepper.

Spread onion in roasting pan; place roast on onion. Spread top of roast with remaining flourless butter mixture; sprinkle with brandy (if using).

Roast in 350°F (180°C) oven, basting often with pan juices after first 30 minutes, until instant-read thermometer inserted in centre reads 140°F (60°C) for medium-rare, about 1½ hours.

Transfer roast to cutting board; tent with foil. Let stand for 10 to 15 minutes before carving into thin slices.

Meanwhile, in saucepan, bring broth, sherry and ⅓ cup water to boil over medium heat. Add mushrooms and remaining salt; return to boil. Reduce heat and simmer until mushrooms are tender, 6 to 8 minutes. Reserving cooking liquid, drain mushrooms.

Stir cooking liquid into roasting pan; bring to boil over medium heat, stirring and scraping up browned bits. Strain into saucepan and bring to boil; whisk in reserved flour-butter mixture and return to simmer, whisking constantly.

Add mushrooms and any accumulated juices from roast; simmer for 2 minutes. Stir in parsley and mustard. Serve with beef.

Makes 12 to 16 servings. PER EACH OF 16 SERVINGS: about 203 cal, 26 g pro, 9 g total fat (5 g sat. fat), 3 g carb, 1 g fibre, 73 mg chol, 335 mg sodium. % RDI: 1% calcium, 21% iron, 6% vit A, 3% vit C, 6% folate.

STANDING RIB ROAST

This gorgeous roast couldn't be easier to prepare. For just five minutes of work, you get a spectacular dinner party entrée, especially if you ask your butcher to french the bone ends for you.

Place roast, bone side down, on rack in roasting pan. Mash garlic with salt to form paste; stir in oil and pepper. Spread over roast.

Roast in 325°F (160°C) oven until instant-read thermometer inserted in centre reads 140°F (60°C) for medium-rare, about 2½ hours.

Transfer roast to cutting board; tent with foil. Let stand for 15 minutes before carving.

GRAVY: Meanwhile, skim off fat from pan juices. Whisk in flour. Place pan over medium heat; whisk in broth, salt and pepper, scraping up browned bits. Bring to boil; reduce heat and simmer until slightly thickened, about 3 minutes. Strain and serve with beef.

8 lb (3.6 kg) **3-rib beef standing rib premium oven roast**

10 cloves **garlic,** minced

2½ tsp **salt** or kosher salt

2 tbsp **vegetable oil**

1 tsp **pepper**

GRAVY:

2 tbsp **all-purpose flour**

2 cups **beef broth**

½ tsp each **salt** and **pepper**

Big beef roasts like this one usually come out of the oven or off the barbecue 5°F (1°C) cooler than their final doneness temperature. Tenting them with foil on a cutting board and letting them stand for 10 to 20 minutes before serving brings them up the final 5°F (1°C) and locks in all the delicious juices.

Makes about 10 servings. PER SERVING: about 601 cal, 50 g pro, 42 g total fat (18 g sat. fat), 2 g carb, trace fibre, 139 mg chol, 910 mg sodium. % RDI: 2% calcium, 31% iron, 2% vit C, 7% folate.

ROAST PRIME RIB WITH ROSEMARY RED WINE JUS LIÉ

Prime rib is so good it doesn't need much dressing up. But *jus lié* – a flavourful sauce made by slightly thickening a blend of the pan juices, wine and broth – adds a touch of sheer elegance to this special-occasion dish. For a dramatic presentation, choose a roast with at least three ribs.

On cutting board, mix thyme with garlic; sprinkle with salt. With side of chef's knife, chop and rub to form smooth paste. Mix in pepper and cayenne pepper; rub all over roast. Wrap in plastic wrap and refrigerate for 4 hours. *(Make-ahead: Refrigerate for up to 24 hours.)*

Scatter onions and rosemary in greased roasting pan. Place roast, bone side down, on onion mixture. Roast in 325°F (160°C) oven until instant-read thermometer inserted in centre reads 140°F (60°C) for medium-rare, 1¾ to 2 hours, or 155°F (68°C) for medium, 2¼ to 2½ hours. Transfer roast to cutting board or platter; tent with foil and let stand for 10 to 15 minutes.

Meanwhile, skim off fat from pan juices; place pan over high heat. Add wine; cook, scraping up any browned bits, until reduced by half, about 3 minutes. Whisk broth with cornstarch; whisk into pan. Bring to boil; boil for 1 minute. Stir in butter. Strain into gravy boat.

Slice bones off meat and separate each rib. Slice meat and arrange on platter along with ribs. Serve with gravy.

2 tbsp chopped **fresh thyme** (or 2 tsp dried)

3 cloves **garlic,** minced

½ tsp **salt**

¼ tsp **pepper**

Pinch **cayenne pepper**

5 to 7 lb (2.25 to 3.15 kg) **beef prime rib premium oven roast**

2 **onions,** thickly sliced

4 sprigs **fresh rosemary**

1 cup **dry red wine**

¾ cup **beef broth**

2 tsp **cornstarch**

2 tbsp **butter**

Makes 8 to 10 servings. PER EACH OF 10 SERVINGS: about 297 cal, 32 g pro, 15 g total fat (7 g sat. fat), 3 g carb, trace fibre, 80 mg chol, 276 mg sodium. % RDI: 2% calcium, 21% iron, 2% vit A, 2% vit C, 5% folate.

BARBECUED PORK BELLY

This very hip cut of braising pork is terrific cooked in the oven, but when it's done on the barbecue, it's a real thing of beauty. To keep the skin supercrisp, don't tent the pork with foil when it comes off the grill. Thickly slice and enjoy with a light salad to complement the rich meat.

2½ to 3 lb (1.125 to 1.35 kg) **whole raw pork belly**

4 **bay leaves,** crumbled

1 tbsp packed **brown sugar**

1 tbsp **smoked paprika**

1 tbsp **ground cumin**

2 tsp **coarse kosher salt**

1 tsp **ground coriander**

1 tsp **cracked pepper**

1 tsp **hot pepper flakes**

Chopped **fresh cilantro**

Pat pork belly dry with paper towel; cut several vertical slashes just through fat layer, about ½ inch (1 cm) apart.

Mix together bay leaves, brown sugar, paprika, cumin, salt, coriander, pepper and hot pepper flakes; sprinkle over meaty side of pork belly. Cover tightly with plastic wrap; refrigerate for 4 hours. *(Make-ahead: Refrigerate for up to 2 days.)* Let stand at room temperature for 30 minutes before grilling.

Set foil drip pan under 1 rack of 2-burner barbecue or under centre rack of 3-burner barbecue. Heat remaining burner(s) to medium. Place pork belly on greased grill over drip pan. Grill, covered and skin side up, on greased grill over medium indirect heat until pork is very tender, about 1½ hours.

Transfer, skin side down, to greased grill over direct medium-high heat; grill, uncovered and turning once, until skin is golden and crisp.

Transfer pork belly to cutting board; let stand for 10 minutes before slicing. Serve garnished with cilantro.

Makes 10 to 12 servings. PER EACH OF 12 SERVINGS: about 418 cal, 9 g pro, 41 g total fat (14 g sat. fat), 2 g carb, 1 g fibre, 58 mg chol, 289 mg sodium, 208 mg potassium. % RDI: 2% calcium, 9% iron, 4% vit A, 2% vit C, 1% folate.

GARLIC ROAST BEEF & GRAVY

Cook this classic Sunday roast in a roasting pan that's big enough to let the air circulate around the meat but not so large that the drippings scorch. This garlicky masterpiece is lovely served with Honey-Glazed Carrots (opposite) and Roasted Accordion New Potatoes (page 227).

3 lb (1.35 kg) **beef top sirloin premium oven roast**

5 cloves **garlic,** minced

1 tsp **salt**

1 tbsp **vegetable oil**

¾ tsp **pepper**

¼ tsp **dried thyme**

¼ cup **dry red wine**

2 cups **sodium-reduced beef broth**

2 tbsp **all-purpose flour**

Place roast, fat side up, on rack in roasting pan. Mash garlic with salt until paste; stir in oil, ½ tsp of the pepper and thyme. Rub all over roast.

Roast in 450°F (230°C) oven for 25 minutes. Reduce heat to 325°F (160°C); roast until instant-read thermometer inserted in centre reads 140°F (60°C) for medium-rare, about 1 hour and 20 minutes. Transfer roast to cutting board; tent with foil. Let stand for 10 minutes before carving.

Meanwhile, place pan over medium-high heat. Add wine, stirring and scraping up browned bits. Add broth, remaining pepper and accumulated juices from roast; bring to simmer, stirring often.

Whisk flour with ¼ cup water; whisk into pan and bring to boil, whisking constantly. Reduce heat and simmer until thickened, about 3 minutes. Strain and serve with beef.

Makes 8 servings. PER SERVING: about 276 cal, 35 g pro, 12 g total fat (4 g sat. fat), 3 g carb, trace fibre, 89 mg chol, 852 mg sodium. % RDI: 2% calcium, 29% iron, 2% vit C, 5% folate.

HONEY-GLAZED CARROTS

Naturally sweet carrots are utterly indulgent when cooked in schmaltz, or rendered animal fat. Look for ready-made schmaltz at the butcher counter. If you can't find any, just substitute the same amount of butter for it. This recipe makes enough for a holiday crowd, but you can halve it for a smaller group.

Cut carrots in half lengthwise; cut crosswise into 1½-inch (4 cm) slices.

In large skillet, heat schmaltz over medium-high heat; cook shallots, stirring often, until softened, about 3 minutes. Add carrots, tossing to coat; cook until slightly softened, about 5 minutes.

Add ¾ cup water, honey and thyme; cook until no liquid remains, about 5 minutes.

Stir in ½ cup water; cook, stirring, until carrots are tender and no liquid remains, 3 to 5 minutes. Sprinkle with salt and pepper; toss to combine.

5 lb (2.25 kg) **carrots** (about 4 bunches), trimmed and peeled

1 tbsp **chicken schmaltz** or beef schmaltz

2 **shallots,** finely diced

2 tbsp **liquid honey**

1 tbsp chopped **fresh thyme**

½ tsp each **salt** and **pepper**

Makes 12 servings. PER SERVING: about 74 cal, 1 g pro, 1 g total fat (trace sat. fat), 15 g carb, 4 g fibre, 1 mg chol, 182 mg sodium, 356 mg potassium. % RDI: 4% calcium, 4% iron, 253% vit A, 10% vit C, 10% folate.

ROTISSERIE BEEF

**For a summer barbecue, serve up slices of this easy roast on kaiser rolls or onion buns.
Since beef eye of round is less tender than premium cuts, marinating and gentle rotisserie cooking
help keep the meat juicy and flavourful.**

¾ cup **dry red wine**

⅓ cup **Dijon mustard**

2 tbsp **red wine vinegar**

1 tbsp each **vegetable oil** and
   sodium-reduced soy sauce

2 tsp **coarsely ground pepper**

4 cloves **garlic,** minced

4 large sprigs **fresh thyme**

1 **onion,** thinly sliced

6 lb (2.7 kg) **beef eye of round
   oven roast**

TIP

This recipe works very well with other
rotisserie roasts – such as sirloin tip,
outside round, inside round and cross rib
– of the same weight. Times may vary
slightly, so watch closely for doneness
clues as you go and test the meat with an
instant-read thermometer.

In large baking dish, whisk together
wine, mustard, vinegar, oil, soy sauce
and pepper. Stir in garlic, thyme and
onion. Add roast, turning to coat.
Cover and refrigerate for 6 hours.
*(Make-ahead: Refrigerate for up to
24 hours.)*

Reserving marinade, drain roast.
Clamp 1 end of roast with rotisserie
fork; insert spit and clamp into
other end.

Follow manufacturer's instructions for
using rotisserie. Or, for 3-burner
barbecue, remove grill racks. Place foil
drip pan along centre of barbecue.
Pour water into pan to depth of 1 inch
(2.5 cm). Heat barbecue to medium-
high. Turn centre burner off. Place
roast on barbecue, centring over drip
pan. Start rotisserie.

Reduce heat to medium; grill,
covered, for 30 minutes.

Meanwhile, strain marinade into small
saucepan and bring to boil; reduce
heat and simmer for 10 minutes.

Brush roast with some of the cooked
marinade; grill for 30 minutes,
brushing with remaining marinade.
Grill until instant-read thermometer
inserted in centre reads 140°F (60°C)
for medium-rare, about 30 minutes.

Transfer roast to cutting board; pull
out forks and spit. Tent with foil; let
stand for 20 minutes before carving
into thin slices.

Makes 12 servings. PER SERVING: about 304 cal, 44 g pro, 12 g total fat (5 g sat. fat), 1 g carb,
trace fibre, 90 mg chol, 230 mg sodium. % RDI: 2% calcium, 23% iron, 5% folate.

LEMONGRASS PORK TENDERLOIN WITH STIR-FRIED QUINOA

Daikon radish has a very pungent aroma, but its crunchy sweetness works well when pickled. If it's not your thing, you can substitute the same amount of carrot. This recipe is a great way to use up leftover quinoa; if you don't have any on hand, make it ahead and spread it out on a large rimmed baking sheet to cool quickly.

Trim dry ends off lemongrass and discard tough outer leaves; slice lemongrass. In blender, purée together lemongrass, green onions, garlic, ¼ cup water, brown sugar, fish sauce and vinegar to form thin paste.

Trim any fat or silverskin off pork; place pork in shallow dish. Pour lemongrass mixture over top, turning to coat; cover and refrigerate for 2 hours. *(Make-ahead: Refrigerate for up to 24 hours.)*

PICKLED RADISH SALAD: Meanwhile, in bowl, whisk together vinegar, sugar and salt; stir in carrot and daikon. Cover and refrigerate for 2 hours. *(Make-ahead: Refrigerate for up to 24 hours.)*

In large nonstick skillet, heat oil over medium-high heat; brown pork all over, about 8 minutes.

Transfer to foil-lined rimmed baking sheet; roast in 375°F (190°C) oven until juices run clear when pork is pierced and just a hint of pink remains inside, or instant-read thermometer inserted in thickest part reads 160°F (71°C), about 35 minutes.

Transfer pork to cutting board; tent with foil. Let stand for 5 minutes before slicing.

STIR-FRIED QUINOA: Meanwhile, in large nonstick skillet or wok, heat oil over medium-high heat; cook garlic, ginger and coriander until fragrant, about 1 minute. Add Swiss chard; cook until wilted, about 2 minutes. Add quinoa, salt and pepper; cook, stirring occasionally, until heated through, about 5 minutes.

Serve quinoa topped with pork and radish salad.

1 stalk **lemongrass**

2 **green onions,** sliced

2 cloves **garlic**

1 tbsp packed **brown sugar**

1 tbsp **fish sauce**

1 tbsp **unseasoned rice vinegar**

1 lb (450 g) **pork tenderloin**

1 tsp **vegetable oil**

STIR-FRIED QUINOA:

1 tbsp **vegetable oil**

3 cloves **garlic,** minced

1 tsp minced **fresh ginger**

1 tsp **ground coriander**

8 cups sliced **Swiss chard leaves and stems** (about 1 bunch)

3 cups cold cooked **quinoa** (about 1 cup uncooked)

½ tsp each **salt** and **pepper**

PICKLED RADISH SALAD:

2 tbsp **unseasoned rice vinegar**

1 tsp **granulated sugar**

Pinch **salt**

1 cup julienned **carrot**

1 cup julienned **daikon radish**

Makes 6 servings. PER SERVING: about 222 cal, 21 g pro, 6 g total fat (1 g sat. fat), 23 g carb, 3 g fibre, 41 mg chol, 560 mg sodium, 791 mg potassium. % RDI: 6% calcium, 29% iron, 52% vit A, 25% vit C, 14% folate.

PORK TENDERLOIN WITH STICKY LIME GLAZE

Sour, salty, sweet and hot flavours dress up a humble pork tenderloin, making it
well suited to easy entertaining. Use a rasp to grate the lime zest – it makes fine shreds
without digging into the bitter white pith.

In large glass bowl, whisk together soy sauce, honey, lime zest, lime juice, onion, ginger, garlic and pepper. *(Make-ahead: Cover and refrigerate for up to 24 hours.)*

Add pork, turning to coat. Cover and refrigerate for 1 hour.

Reserving marinade, drain pork. In large ovenproof skillet, heat oil over medium-high heat; brown pork. Pour in marinade and bring to boil; boil for 1 minute.

Roast in 400°F (200°C) oven until juices run clear when pork is pierced and just a hint of pink remains inside, or instant-read thermometer inserted in thickest part reads 160°F (71°C), about 18 minutes.

Transfer pork to cutting board; tent with foil. Let stand for 5 minutes before slicing. Arrange on platter; pour sauce over top.

¼ cup **sodium-reduced soy sauce**

¼ cup **liquid honey**

2 tsp grated **lime zest**

3 tbsp **lime juice**

1 small **onion,** finely diced

2 tbsp minced **fresh ginger**

2 cloves **garlic,** minced

½ tsp **pepper**

2 **pork tenderloins** (about 12 oz/ 340 g each)

1 tbsp **vegetable oil**

Makes 6 servings. PER SERVING: about 222 cal, 28 g pro, 5 g total fat (1 g sat. fat), 16 g carb,
1 g fibre, 67 mg chol, 413 mg sodium. % RDI: 1% calcium, 13% iron, 7% vit C, 5% folate.

PANCETTA-WRAPPED PORK TENDERLOIN WITH GARLIC MASHED POTATOES

How do you keep a lean roast moist and juicy?
Wrap it in peppery pancetta, of course! The garlic mashed potatoes are
a slam-dunk side with this and many other roasts.

1 tbsp **olive oil**

1 clove **garlic,** minced

½ tsp each **dried sage** and **pepper**

12 oz (340 g) **pork tenderloin**

8 thin slices **pancetta**

GARLIC MASHED POTATOES:
2 lb (900 g) **yellow-fleshed potatoes,** peeled and cubed

4 cloves **garlic**

½ cup **milk**

2 tbsp **butter**

¼ tsp **salt**

Stir together oil, garlic, sage and pepper; rub all over pork. Place pork on foil-lined or parchment paper–lined rimmed baking sheet; wrap with pancetta, overlapping slices.

Roast in 425°F (220°C) oven until juices run clear when pork is pierced and just a hint of pink remains inside, or instant-read thermometer inserted in thickest part reads 160°F (71°C), 15 to 18 minutes.

Transfer pork to cutting board; let stand for 5 minutes before slicing.

GARLIC MASHED POTATOES: Meanwhile, in large pot of boiling lightly salted water, cook potatoes with garlic until tender, 10 to 15 minutes. Drain and return to pot; mash in milk, butter and salt. Serve with pork.

Makes 4 servings. PER SERVING: about 437 cal, 29 g pro, 18 g total fat (7 g sat. fat), 39 g carb, 3 g fibre, 89 mg chol, 1,037 mg sodium, 924 mg potassium. % RDI: 6% calcium, 12% iron, 7% vit A, 25% vit C, 10% folate.

MISO-GLAZED PORK TENDERLOIN

Miso, also known as soybean paste, comes in a few varieties – the white and red ones are the most delicious for this simple pork roast. Look for miso in the Asian aisle of the grocery store. It keeps for a very long time in the fridge; use up leftovers in soups and other marinades.

2 tbsp **red miso paste** or yellow miso paste

2 tbsp **liquid honey**

2 cloves **garlic,** minced

1 tsp **unseasoned rice vinegar**

½ tsp **sesame oil**

1 lb (450 g) **pork tenderloin**

Pinch **pepper**

2 tsp **vegetable oil**

In small saucepan, bring miso paste, honey, garlic, vinegar, sesame oil and ¾ cup water to boil; reduce heat and simmer until reduced to ⅓ cup, about 8 minutes.

Meanwhile, trim any silverskin off pork; sprinkle pork with pepper. In large ovenproof skillet, heat vegetable oil over medium-high heat; sear pork until browned all over, about 7 minutes.

Brush 1 tbsp of the miso mixture over pork. Roast in 400°F (200°C) oven until juices run clear when pork is pierced and just a hint of pink remains inside, or instant-read thermometer inserted in thickest part reads 160°F (71°C), about 16 minutes.

Transfer pork to cutting board; let stand for 5 minutes before slicing. Drizzle remaining miso mixture over pork before serving.

Makes 4 servings. PER SERVING: about 203 cal, 26 g pro, 6 g total fat (1 g sat. fat), 12 g carb, 1 g fibre, 61 mg chol, 372 mg sodium, 383 mg potassium. % RDI: 1% calcium, 10% iron, 2% vit C, 3% folate.

PEACH CHIPOTLE PORK WITH ASPARAGUS

The chipotles in the glaze add a fun, spicy kick to this roast. Seeding them allows the flavour to come through with less heat. Chipotle peppers freeze well, so once you open a can, store any leftovers in an airtight container in the freezer.

In small saucepan over medium-high heat, bring jam, vinegar, garlic and chipotles to boil; cook, stirring occasionally, until jam is melted, about 2 minutes. Set aside 2 tbsp for glaze.

Sprinkle pork with pinch each of the salt and pepper. Brush remaining jam mixture all over pork. Grill, covered, on greased grill over medium-high heat, turning occasionally, until juices run clear when pork is pierced and just a hint of pink remains inside, or instant-read thermometer inserted in thickest part reads 160°F (71°C), about 18 minutes.

Transfer pork to cutting board; let stand for 5 minutes before slicing. Drizzle pork with reserved glaze.

Meanwhile, toss together asparagus, oil, and remaining salt and pepper. Add to grill; cook, covered and turning occasionally, until tender-crisp, 7 minutes. Serve with pork.

⅓ cup **peach jam**

3 tbsp **white wine vinegar**

2 cloves **garlic,** chopped

2 **canned chipotle peppers in adobo sauce,** drained, seeded and chopped

1 lb (450 g) **pork tenderloin**

¼ tsp each **salt** and **pepper**

1 bunch (9 oz/255 g) **asparagus,** trimmed

1 tbsp **olive oil**

Makes 4 servings. PER SERVING: about 250 cal, 26 g pro, 6 g total fat (2 g sat. fat), 22 g carb, 1 g fibre, 61 mg chol, 253 mg sodium, 486 mg potassium. % RDI: 3% calcium, 14% iron, 8% vit A, 12% vit C, 34% folate.

PEACH CHIPOTLE PORK WITH ASPARAGUS page 163

SICILIAN STUFFED PORK TENDERLOIN

Inspired by the classic southern Italian combination of bread crumbs, pine nuts and currants plus caramelized onions, this stuffed roast is sure to please. If you prefer, substitute an equal amount of chopped walnuts for the pine nuts.

2 **pork tenderloins** (about 2 lb/ 900 g total)

2 tbsp each **Dijon mustard** and **liquid honey**

1 tbsp **extra-virgin olive oil**

¼ tsp each **salt** and **pepper**

STUFFING:

2 tbsp **butter**

3 **onions,** thinly sliced

¼ cup **dried currants**

1 tbsp **balsamic vinegar**

¼ tsp each **salt** and **pepper**

⅓ cup **fresh bread crumbs**

¼ cup toasted **pine nuts**

3 tbsp chopped **fresh parsley**

1 tsp grated **orange zest**

1 tbsp **orange juice**

STUFFING: In skillet, melt butter over medium-low heat; fry onions, stirring occasionally, until deep golden, about 20 minutes. Stir in currants, vinegar, salt and pepper; cook for 5 minutes. Remove from heat. Stir in bread crumbs, pine nuts, parsley, orange zest and orange juice.

Starting at thick end of each tenderloin, insert handle of wooden spoon lengthwise through centre almost but not all the way through to make pocket. Fill with stuffing, using handle to gently push stuffing evenly into pockets. *(Make-ahead: Wrap and refrigerate for up to 24 hours.)* Place on greased rimmed baking sheet or in greased small roasting pan.

Combine mustard, honey, oil, salt and pepper; brush over pork. Roast in 400°F (200°C) oven until juices run clear when pork is pierced and just a hint of pink remains inside, or instant-read thermometer inserted in thickest part reads 160°F (71°C), about 40 minutes.

Transfer pork to cutting board; tent with foil. Let stand for 10 minutes before slicing.

Makes 4 to 6 servings. PER EACH OF 6 SERVINGS: about 298 cal, 30 g pro, 13 g total fat (4 g sat. fat), 15 g carb, 2 g fibre, 73 mg chol, 363 mg sodium. % RDI: 3% calcium, 18% iron, 5% vit A, 22% vit C, 10% folate.

APRICOT & RED PEPPER PORK TENDERLOIN

Here, apricots and hot pepper flakes pair up to create the perfect balance of sweet and spicy. Multigrain bread crumbs are a nutty change from regular white ones – whirl leftover bread in the food processor and freeze any extras whenever you have the chance.

In large skillet, heat 2 tsp of the oil over medium-high heat; cook onion and red pepper, stirring occasionally, until softened, about 3 minutes.

Add apricots, bread crumbs and hot pepper flakes; cook for 1 minute. Stir in 2 tbsp water, parsley and pinch each of the salt and pepper.

On cutting board, cut pork horizontally in half almost but not all the way through; open like book. Using meat mallet, pound to even thickness. Mound stuffing lengthwise along centre; fold pork over stuffing and tie at intervals with kitchen string. Sprinkle with remaining salt and pepper.

In ovenproof skillet, heat remaining oil over medium-high heat; brown pork all over, 7 to 8 minutes. Roast in 400°F (200°C) oven until juices run clear when pork is pierced and just a hint of pink remains inside, or instant-read thermometer inserted in thickest part reads 160°F (71°C), 15 to 20 minutes.

Mix mustard with honey; brush over pork.

4 tsp **olive oil**

⅓ cup diced **red onion**

⅓ cup diced **sweet red pepper**

5 **dried apricots,** finely chopped

½ cup **fresh multigrain bread crumbs** or fresh whole wheat bread crumbs

Pinch **hot pepper flakes**

1 tbsp chopped **fresh parsley**

¼ tsp each **salt** and **pepper**

1 lb (450 g) **pork tenderloin**

1 tbsp **Dijon mustard**

1 tbsp **liquid honey**

Makes 4 servings. PER SERVING: about 225 cal, 27 g pro, 7 g total fat (1 g sat. fat), 15 g carb, 2 g fibre, 63 mg chol, 282 mg sodium, 593 mg potassium. % RDI: 3% calcium, 14% iron, 9% vit A, 38% vit C, 6% folate.

ROAST PORK WITH CIDER CREAM SAUCE

A golden crust and apple-flavoured sauce make this an ideal entertaining main. Choose a long, slender roast (rather than a short, thick one) because it will be easier to slice and look more attractive when served.

2 tbsp **vegetable oil**

3 cloves **garlic,** minced

1 tbsp each minced **fresh sage** and **fresh thyme** (or ½ tsp each crumbled dried)

1 tsp **salt**

½ tsp **pepper**

3 lb (1.35 kg) **boneless pork loin centre roast,** rolled and tied

CIDER CREAM:

2 tbsp **butter**

2 **Granny Smith apples,** peeled, quartered and thinly sliced crosswise

1 **onion,** diced

1 cup **apple cider** (alcoholic or nonalcoholic)

1 cup **sodium-reduced chicken broth**

¾ cup **whipping cream (35%)**

1 tbsp **grainy mustard** or Dijon mustard

1 tsp **cornstarch**

Mix together oil, garlic, sage, thyme, salt and pepper; rub all over roast. Cover and refrigerate for 2 hours. *(Make-ahead: Refrigerate for up to 24 hours.)*

Place pork on rack in roasting pan. Roast in 375°F (190°C) oven until juices run clear when pork is pierced and just a hint of pink remains inside, or instant-read thermometer inserted in thickest part reads 160°F (71°C), about 1½ hours.

Transfer pork to cutting board; tent with foil. Let stand for 15 minutes before slicing.

CIDER CREAM: Meanwhile, skim off fat from pan juices. Add butter; melt over medium heat. Fry apples and onion, stirring often, for 5 minutes. Add cider and bring to boil, scraping up any browned bits. Stir in broth, cream and mustard; boil until reduced by half, about 8 minutes.

Stir cornstarch with 1 tbsp cold water; whisk into sauce and cook, whisking, until thickened, about 1 minute. Serve with pork.

Makes 8 servings. PER SERVING: about 397 cal, 34 g pro, 23 g total fat (10 g sat. fat), 11 g carb, 1 g fibre, 128 mg chol, 493 mg sodium. % RDI: 6% calcium, 11% iron, 10% vit A, 5% vit C, 4% folate.

PORK & NAPA SALAD

A lime-and-ginger-infused cabbage salad is the ideal complement to this Asian-inspired pork. To make shredding the cabbage much easier, use the shredder blade in your food processor.

1 tbsp **vegetable oil**

2 cloves **garlic,** minced

½ tsp each **salt** and **pepper**

½ tsp **ground coriander**

¼ tsp **ground cloves**

1 lb (450 g) **pork tenderloin**

6 cups shredded **napa cabbage** (about 1 small)

1 **carrot,** julienned

1 cup **sugar snap peas,** blanched and halved

2 **green onions,** thinly sliced

2 tbsp **lime juice**

1 tbsp **sesame oil**

1 tbsp **vinegar**

1 tbsp **fish sauce**

2 tsp **granulated sugar**

2 tsp minced **fresh ginger**

Stir together vegetable oil, garlic, salt, pepper, coriander and cloves; brush over pork. Let stand for 15 minutes.

Grill pork, covered, on greased grill over medium-high heat, turning 3 times, until juices run clear when pork is pierced and just a hint of pink remains inside, or instant-read thermometer inserted in thickest part reads 160°F (71°C), 15 to 20 minutes.

Transfer pork to cutting board; tent with foil. Let stand for 5 minutes before slicing.

Meanwhile, toss together cabbage, carrot, peas, green onions, lime juice, sesame oil, vinegar, fish sauce, sugar and ginger until coated. Divide among plates. Top with pork.

Barbecues are all different, so it pays to get to know the one you have – yours might burn hotter or cooler than the gauge says. Watch your food carefully as it cooks. "If meat is browning too quickly (or not quickly enough), adjust the temperature accordingly. An inexpensive oven thermometer is a handy tool to have inside the barbecue – keep your eye on it as you cook and play with the heat to maintain the right level.

Makes 4 servings. PER SERVING: about 247 cal, 28 g pro, 10 g total fat (2 g sat. fat), 13 g carb, 3 g fibre, 61 mg chol, 715 mg sodium. % RDI: 11% calcium, 16% iron, 31% vit A, 68% vit C, 53% folate.

PORK WITH SPICY-SWEET PEPPER SAUCE FOR TWO

**A roast for just two? You bet, and it's as easy as one, two, done.
This tenderloin can be on the table in 40 minutes if you prep the sauce while the pork roasts.**

Sprinkle pork with garlic, ginger, salt and pepper; let stand for 10 minutes.

In ovenproof skillet, heat oil over medium-high heat; sear pork all over, about 5 minutes.

Roast in 400°F (200°C) oven until juices run clear when pork is pierced and just a hint of pink remains inside, or instant-read thermometer inserted in thickest part reads 160°F (71°C), 15 to 20 minutes.

Transfer pork to cutting board; tent with foil. Let stand for 5 minutes before slicing.

SAUCE: Meanwhile, in small saucepan, heat oil over medium heat; cook sweet pepper, hot pepper and garlic until tender, about 3 minutes. Stir in chili sauce, brown sugar, vinegar, soy sauce and ginger; simmer, stirring, until reduced to ½ cup, about 4 minutes. Stir in green onion. Pour sauce over pork to serve.

12 oz (340 g) **pork tenderloin**
1 clove **garlic,** minced
¼ tsp grated **fresh ginger**
¼ tsp each **salt** and **pepper**
2 tsp **vegetable oil**

SAUCE:
2 tsp **vegetable oil**
Quarter **sweet red pepper,** sliced
1 **red finger hot pepper,** sliced
1 clove **garlic,** minced
3 tbsp **smooth Thai chili sauce**
1 tbsp packed **brown sugar**
1 tbsp each **unseasoned rice vinegar** and **sodium-reduced soy sauce**
1 tsp minced **fresh ginger**
1 **green onion,** chopped

Makes 2 servings. PER SERVING: about 401 cal, 45 g pro, 13 g total fat (2 g sat. fat), 22 g carb, 1 g fibre, 107 mg chol, 863 mg sodium, 803 mg potassium. % RDI: 3% calcium, 21% iron, 9% vit A, 90% vit C, 10% folate.

ROSEMARY SAGE RACK OF PORK

**A rack of pork looks totally spectacular – your guests never have to know how simple it is to make.
If you want one rib per person, ask the butcher to tie two racks together for you.**

¾ tsp **fennel seeds**

3 tbsp **extra-virgin olive oil**

4 cloves **garlic,** minced

2 tbsp minced **fresh rosemary**

1 tbsp minced **fresh sage**

1 tbsp **lemon juice**

½ tsp each **salt** and **pepper**

3½ lb (1.5 kg) **rack of pork,** backbone removed

In skillet, lightly toast fennel seeds over low heat, about 2 minutes. Let cool. Using bottom of heavy saucepan, gently crush just until broken. Mix together fennel seeds, oil, garlic, rosemary, sage, lemon juice, salt and pepper.

With long sharp knife, cut 2-inch (5 cm) wide slit lengthwise through centre of roast. With wooden spoon handle, stretch hole to form pocket. Using fingers, push about 1 tbsp of the herb mixture into pocket.

Spread remaining herb mixture all over pork. Cover; refrigerate, turning occasionally, for 2 hours. *(Make-ahead: Refrigerate for up to 24 hours.)*

Wrap rib ends in foil to prevent charring. Set foil drip pan under 1 rack of 2-burner barbecue or under centre rack of 3-burner barbecue. Heat remaining burner(s) to medium. Place pork on greased grill over drip pan; grill, covered and turning every 20 minutes, until juices run clear when pork is pierced and just a hint of pink remains inside, or instant-read thermometer inserted in centre reads 160°F (71°C), 1½ to 2 hours.

Transfer pork to cutting board; tent with foil. Let stand for 15 minutes before slicing between ribs.

Makes 6 to 8 servings. PER EACH OF 8 SERVINGS: about 250 cal, 26 g pro, 15 g total fat (5 g sat. fat), 1 g carb, trace fibre, 64 mg chol, 187 mg sodium. % RDI: 3% calcium, 7% iron, 2% vit C, 1% folate.

CHANGE IT UP

Oven-Roasted Rosemary Sage Rack of Pork

Prepare pork as directed; place on greased rack in roasting pan. Roast in 325°F (160°C) oven, basting with pan juices every 30 minutes, until juices run clear when pork is pierced and just a hint of pink remains inside, or instant-read thermometer inserted in centre reads 160°F (71°C), 1½ hours.

ROAST PORK LOIN WITH PORT & PRUNES

**The Douro region of Portugal is famous for both its wine and its meat –
tasty veal and black pork, served with roasted or fried potatoes.
This prune-studded roast is inspired by a typical Douro recipe.**

8 **pitted prunes,** halved

¼ cup **ruby Port** or tawny Port

2 cloves **garlic,** minced

1¼ tsp **salt**

3 lb (1.35 kg) **boneless pork loin
centre roast**

¾ tsp **sweet paprika**

¼ cup **extra-virgin olive oil**

Mix together prunes, Port, garlic and
½ tsp of the salt; let stand for 1 hour.

Cut 16 slits all over pork at even
intervals; insert prune half with
clinging garlic into each slit. Place
pork in roasting pan; sprinkle with
paprika and remaining salt. Mix
prune juices with oil; spoon 3 tbsp
over pork.

Roast in 325°F (160°C) oven, basting
often with oil mixture and later with
pan juices, until juices run clear when
pork is pierced and just a hint of pink
remains inside, or instant-read
thermometer inserted in centre reads
160°F (71°C), 1 to 1½ hours.

Reserving pan juices, transfer pork
to serving platter; tent with foil.
Let stand for 10 minutes before
thinly slicing.

Mix carving juices with pan juices;
serve with pork.

To butterfly a pork roast (opposite), place roast, fat side up, on cutting
board. Starting ½ inch (1 cm) from bottom, make 1-inch (2.5 cm) deep
horizontal cut along length. Keeping knife parallel to cutting board to
maintain ½-inch (1 cm) thickness, cut deeper into roast, pushing away
or "unrolling" meat as you cut. Repeat until you've sliced through
entire roast to form a 12- x 10-inch (30 x 25 cm) flat rectangle.

Makes 8 servings. PER SERVING: about 380 cal, 38 g pro, 21 g total fat (7 g sat. fat), 7 g carb,
1 g fibre, 92 mg chol, 443 mg sodium, 653 mg potassium. % RDI: 1% calcium, 9% iron, 2% vit A,
3% vit C, 3% folate.

ARTICHOKE-STUFFED PORK LOIN WITH LEMONY ROASTED ROOT VEGETABLES

Stuffing a roast with moist, flavourful ingredients keeps the meat juicy – and makes it a guaranteed showstopper when you bring it to the table to carve. Mozzarella or Fontina cheese is a nice substitute for the Gouda if you prefer.

In Dutch oven, cover and cook spinach with 2 tbsp water over medium-high heat, stirring once, until wilted, about 2 minutes. Drain in sieve, pressing out moisture. Transfer to bowl; let cool.

In same pan, heat 2 tbsp of the oil over medium heat; cook garlic and leek, stirring, until softened, 4 to 6 minutes. Add to spinach along with artichokes, Gouda cheese, bread crumbs, Parmesan cheese, parsley and ¼ tsp each of the salt and pepper; toss to combine. *(Make-ahead: Cover and refrigerate for up to 24 hours.)*

Open pork roast flat; mound spinach mixture down centre. Fold pork in half to cover. Place four 17-inch (43 cm) pieces kitchen string crosswise under pork; tie at top, cutting off excess. Brush with remaining oil; sprinkle with remaining salt and pepper. Transfer to roasting pan.

LEMONY ROASTED ROOT VEGETABLES:
In bowl, whisk oil, oregano, lemon juice, mustard, salt, pepper and hot pepper flakes. Add potatoes, carrots and onion; toss to coat. Arrange around pork. *(Make-ahead: Cover and refrigerate for up to 12 hours.)*

Roast in 400°F (200°C) oven, basting 3 times with pan juices, until juices run clear when pork is pierced and just a hint of pink remains inside, or instant-read thermometer inserted in centre reads 160°F (71°C), about 1¼ hours.

Transfer pork to cutting board; tent with foil. Let stand for 20 minutes before cutting into 8 slices.

Meanwhile, continue roasting vegetables until potatoes are browned and tender, about 25 minutes. Serve with pork.

5 oz (140 g) **fresh baby spinach**

3 tbsp **olive oil**

3 cloves **garlic,** minced

1 **leek** (white and light green parts only), thinly sliced (about 2½ cups)

1 can (398 mL) **artichoke hearts,** drained, pressed to remove liquid and chopped

1 cup shredded **Gouda cheese**

¾ cup **fresh bread crumbs**

½ cup grated **Parmesan cheese**

⅓ cup chopped **fresh flat-leaf parsley**

½ tsp each **salt** and **pepper**

3 lb (1.35 kg) **boneless pork loin centre roast,** butterflied (see Tip, opposite)

LEMONY ROASTED ROOT VEGETABLES:
¼ cup **extra-virgin olive oil**

3 tbsp chopped **fresh oregano**

3 tbsp **lemon juice**

1 tbsp **Dijon mustard**

½ tsp each **salt** and **pepper**

¼ tsp **hot pepper flakes**

1 lb (450 g) **mini yellow-fleshed potatoes** or yellow fingerling potatoes, scrubbed and halved lengthwise

2 **carrots,** cut diagonally in ½-inch (1 cm) thick slices

1 large **onion,** chopped

Makes 8 servings. PER SERVING: about 507 cal, 47 g pro, 26 g total fat (8 g sat. fat), 22 g carb, 5 g fibre, 105 mg chol, 763 mg sodium, 1,144 mg potassium. % RDI: 23% calcium, 26% iron, 56% vit A, 28% vit C, 37% folate.

PORK TENDERLOIN WITH MUSHROOM PAN SAUCE

Cremini mushrooms have a rich taste and are terrific paired with shallots in this mouthwatering dish. Serve with mashed potatoes or crusty bread to soak up the savoury sauce.

Sprinkle pork with salt and pepper. In skillet, heat oil over medium-high heat; brown pork all over. Transfer to foil-lined rimmed baking sheet; roast in 400°F (200°C) oven until juices run clear when pork is pierced and just a hint of pink remains inside, or instant-read thermometer inserted in thickest part reads 160°F (71°C), about 18 minutes.

Transfer pork to cutting board; let stand for 5 minutes before slicing.

MUSHROOM PAN SAUCE: Meanwhile, in same skillet, heat oil over medium-high heat; sauté shallots until softened, 3 minutes. Add mushrooms, thyme, salt and pepper; sauté until mushrooms are golden, 6 minutes.

Add wine; cook, stirring and scraping up any browned bits, until no liquid remains. Add broth; cook for 5 minutes.

Mash butter with flour and add to sauce along with parsley; simmer, stirring, until thickened. Stir in any accumulated juices from pork. Serve with pork.

---

1 lb (450 g) **pork tenderloin**

¼ tsp each **salt** and **pepper**

1 tbsp **vegetable oil**

MUSHROOM PAN SAUCE:

1 tbsp **vegetable oil**

2 large **shallots,** finely chopped (or 1 small onion, chopped)

8 oz (225 g) **cremini mushrooms,** sliced

¼ tsp **dried thyme**

Pinch each **salt** and **pepper**

¼ cup **dry white wine** or sodium-reduced chicken broth

1 cup **sodium-reduced chicken broth**

1 tbsp **butter,** softened

1 tbsp **all-purpose flour**

3 tbsp chopped **fresh parsley**

Makes 4 servings. PER SERVING: about 259 cal, 29 g pro, 13 g total fat (3 g sat. fat), 5 g carb, 1 g fibre, 75 mg chol, 372 mg sodium. % RDI: 2% calcium, 18% iron, 6% vit A, 10% vit C, 10% folate.

ROAST PORK & SQUASH

When squash is in season in the fall, look for locally grown, interesting varieties to try in this recipe. It's wonderful with almost any type of winter squash.

2 small **squash** (turban, acorn or mini-Hubbard), each about 2½ lb (1.125 kg)

2 tbsp **extra-virgin olive oil**

1 tbsp chopped **fresh rosemary**

¾ tsp **salt**

¾ tsp **pepper**

3 cloves **garlic**

3½ lb (1.5 kg) **pork rib roast**

Cut each squash in half; scrape out seeds. Cut each half into quarters to make 16 pieces total. In large roasting pan, toss squash with 1 tsp each of the oil and rosemary, and ¼ tsp each of the salt and pepper. Push to end of pan.

On cutting board, mince garlic. Using side of chef's knife, rub in remaining salt to make paste. In small bowl, mix with remaining oil, rosemary and pepper. Spread all over pork.

Place pork on greased rack; place in pan and surround with squash. Roast in 375°F (190°C) oven until juices run clear when pork is pierced and just a hint of pink remains inside, or instant-read thermometer inserted in centre reads 160°F (71°C), about 1 hour and 20 minutes.

Transfer pork to cutting board; tent with foil. Let stand for 10 minutes before slicing. Serve with squash.

Makes 6 servings. PER SERVING: about 428 cal, 37 g pro, 18 g total fat (6 g sat. fat), 31 g carb, 4 g fibre, 85 mg chol, 352 mg sodium. % RDI: 12% calcium, 24% iron, 9% vit A, 38% vit C, 20% folate.

CROWN ROAST OF PORK WITH PRUNE & BACON STUFFING

**A crown roast is the perfect cut for tableside carving –
and it's a great value for feeding a crowd in style. You may not be a fan of prunes normally,
but they're so sweet and tender in this recipe that you'll be a convert.**

STUFFING: Soak prunes in apple cider for 30 minutes. Reserving cider, drain prunes. Meanwhile, on baking sheet, bake bread in 400°F (200°C) oven, stirring halfway through, until golden, 8 minutes. Transfer to large bowl.

In skillet, cook bacon over medium-low heat until fat is rendered, 3 to 5 minutes. Drain all but 2 tbsp fat from pan. Stir in onions, celery, salt and cloves; cook over medium heat until softened, 8 to 10 minutes. Stir in reserved cider, scraping up browned bits; cook until slightly thickened, 5 to 8 minutes. Add to bowl along with prunes and parsley; stir to combine.

Using mortar and pestle, or mini-chopper, grind together oil, garlic, savory, salt and pepper until paste; rub all over pork, avoiding bones.

Place pork in foil-lined roasting pan; spoon stuffing into centre. Wrap each exposed rib tip in foil; cover stuffing with foil.

Roast pork in 325°F (160°C) oven until instant-read thermometer inserted in thickest part reads 160°F (71°C), 2½ to 3 hours.

Transfer pork to serving platter; remove foil from stuffing and rib tips. Tent pork with foil; let stand for 20 minutes before slicing between ribs. Serve with stuffing.

2 tbsp **vegetable oil**

3 cloves **garlic**

1 tsp **dried savory**

½ tsp each **salt** and **pepper**

6½ lb (3 kg) **12-rib crown roast of pork**

STUFFING:

¾ cup **pitted prunes,** halved

½ cup **apple cider**

4 cups cubed (½ inch/1 cm) **day-old crustless bread**

5 slices **bacon,** cut in 1-inch (2.5 cm) strips

2 **onions,** diced

1 rib **celery,** diced

½ tsp **salt**

¼ tsp **ground cloves**

¼ cup chopped **fresh parsley**

Makes 12 servings. PER SERVING: about 372 cal, 35 g pro, 18 g total fat (6 g sat. fat), 16 g carb, 2 g fibre, 84 mg chol, 372 mg sodium, 653 mg potassium. % RDI: 5% calcium, 13% iron, 2% vit A, 3% vit C, 9% folate.

PORK PERSILLADE

Persillade is a simple French mixture of parsley and garlic that adds elegance and flavour to large cuts of meat. Serve this roast with seasonal veggies or a side of old-fashioned applesauce.

3½ lb (1.5 kg) **pork rib roast**
½ tsp each **salt** and **pepper**
1½ cups chopped **fresh parsley**
6 cloves **garlic,** minced
2 tbsp **extra-virgin olive oil**

Sprinkle roast all over with salt and pepper. Mix together parsley, garlic and oil until paste; rub all over pork. *(Make-ahead: Cover and refrigerate for up to 24 hours.)*

Place pork on greased rack in roasting pan; roast in 325°F (160°C) oven until juices run clear when pork is pierced and just a hint of pink remains inside, or instant-read thermometer inserted in centre reads 160°F (71°C), about 2 hours.

Transfer pork to cutting board; tent with foil. Let stand for 10 minutes before slicing.

TIP It used to be that you had to cook pork until it was white all the way through – leaving you with dry, woolly meat that wasn't a pleasure to eat. Today, thanks to modern handling and breeding practices, it's safe (and more enjoyable) to eat pork that's cooked until just a hint of pink remains in the centre (160°F/71°C on an instant-read thermometer). Pork is much juicier and more flavourful this way!

Makes 6 servings. PER SERVING: about 362 cal, 39 g pro, 21 g total fat (7 g sat. fat), 2 g carb, 1 g fibre, 105 mg chol, 240 mg sodium. % RDI: 6% calcium, 20% iron, 7% vit A, 30% vit C, 12% folate.

MAPLE, MUSTARD & RIESLING ROAST PORK

This pork roast demands little marinating time and just a couple of quick bastes while it's in the oven. Make sure you enjoy a sip or two of the Riesling while you roast the meat.

In dish large enough to hold pork or in large resealable bag, mix together ¾ cup of the wine, the maple syrup, Dijon mustard, oil, grainy mustard, garlic and pepper. Add pork; turn to coat. Cover and refrigerate, turning once, for 1 hour. *(Make-ahead: Refrigerate for up to 12 hours.)*

Cut shallots into ½-inch (1 cm) thick pieces; place in roasting pan. Top with pork; drizzle with remaining marinade. Roast in 325°F (160°C) oven, basting 2 or 3 times with pan juices, until juices run clear when pork is pierced and just a hint of pink remains inside, or instant-read thermometer inserted in centre reads 160°F (71°C), about 2 hours.

Reserving pan juices, transfer pork and shallots to serving platter; tent with foil. Let stand for 10 minutes before thinly slicing pork.

Place pan over medium heat; bring juices to boil. Add remaining wine; cook, stirring and scraping up any browned bits, for 2 minutes. Mix carving juices into pan juices; serve with pork.

1 cup **Riesling wine**
¼ cup **maple syrup**
3 tbsp **Dijon mustard**
3 tbsp **olive oil**
2 tbsp **grainy mustard**
2 cloves **garlic,** minced
¼ tsp **pepper**
3 lb (1.35 kg) **boneless pork loin centre roast**
8 oz (225 g) **shallots** (about 8 large)

Makes 8 servings. PER SERVING: about 351 cal, 36 g pro, 16 g total fat (5 g sat. fat), 12 g carb, 1 g fibre, 83 mg chol, 196 mg sodium, 678 mg potassium. % RDI: 4% calcium, 12% iron, 3% vit A, 3% vit C, 6% folate.

PROSCIUTTO PESTO PORK FOR TWO

Smoky, herby and satisfying, this lovely stuffed tenderloin is ideal for sharing with someone special. Serve with Oven-Roasted Grape Tomatoes (page 48) and Buttermilk Smashed Potatoes (opposite).

12 oz (340 g) **pork tenderloin**

2 tbsp **sun-dried tomato pesto**

2 oz (55 g) **prosciutto,** thinly sliced

4 large leaves **fresh basil**

3 tbsp shredded **smoked Gouda cheese** or mozzarella cheese

1 tbsp **vegetable oil**

Cut pork lengthwise in half almost but not all the way through; open like book. Spread pesto down centre of 1 side. Lay prosciutto on pesto; top with overlapping basil leaves. Sprinkle with Gouda cheese. Fold pork over filling; secure with toothpicks or kitchen string.

In large ovenproof skillet, heat oil over medium-high heat; brown pork. Roast in 400°F (200°C) oven until juices run clear when pork is pierced and just a hint of pink remains inside, or instant-read thermometer inserted in centre reads 160°F (71°C), about 18 minutes.

Transfer pork to cutting board; tent with foil. Let stand for 10 minutes before slicing.

Makes 2 servings. PER SERVING: about 384 cal, 50 g pro, 18 g total fat (5 g sat. fat), 3 g carb, trace fibre, 119 mg chol, 682 mg sodium. % RDI: 8% calcium, 18% iron, 3% vit A, 2% vit C, 5% folate.

BUTTERMILK SMASHED POTATOES

Buttermilk gives these potatoes a creamy texture and a subtle tang without adding a huge amount of fat. This recipe is easily doubled for a crowd.

In large saucepan of boiling salted water, cover and cook potatoes with garlic until tender, about 15 minutes. Drain and return to pot; dry over low heat, shaking pan occasionally, about 2 minutes. Remove from heat.

Add buttermilk, butter, salt and pepper; smash with potato masher until almost smooth with some large chunks.

1 lb (450 g) **yellow-fleshed potatoes** (about 2), peeled and cut in chunks

1 clove **garlic**

½ cup **buttermilk**

1 tbsp **butter**

¼ tsp **salt**

Pinch **pepper**

Makes 2 servings. PER SERVING: about 249 cal, 6 g pro, 7 g total fat (5 g sat. fat), 41 g carb, 3 g fibre, 20 mg chol, 838 mg sodium. % RDI: 10% calcium, 12% iron, 6% vit A, 40% vit C, 10% folate.

PORCHETTA-STYLE BARBECUE PORK ROAST

Traditional porchetta is slow-roasted with herbs under a crunchy layer of crackling. Here, prosciutto makes the perfect lower-fat alternative to the crackling without sacrificing flavour. Leftovers make a great sandwich filling.

¼ cup chopped **fresh parsley**

1 tbsp each chopped **fresh rosemary** and **fresh sage**

3 cloves **garlic,** pressed or grated

2 tsp **Dijon mustard**

1 tsp **fennel seeds,** crushed

1 tsp grated **lemon zest**

½ tsp **pepper**

Pinch each **salt** and **hot pepper flakes**

1 tbsp **olive oil**

2½ lb (1.125 kg) **boneless pork loin centre roast**

4 slices **prosciutto** (2 oz/55 g total)

In small bowl, combine parsley, rosemary, sage, garlic, mustard, fennel seeds, lemon zest, pepper, salt and hot pepper flakes; stir in oil. Spread over pork. Cover and refrigerate for 1 hour. *(Make-ahead: Refrigerate for up to 24 hours.)*

Overlapping slices, arrange prosciutto over top of pork. With kitchen string, tie pork in 5 or 6 places to secure.

Set foil drip pan under 1 rack of 2-burner barbecue or under centre rack of 3-burner barbecue. Heat remaining burner(s) to medium. Place pork on greased grill over drip pan; grill, covered, until juices run clear when pork is pierced and just a hint of pink remains inside, or instant-read thermometer inserted in centre reads 160°F (71°C), about 1½ hours.

Transfer pork to cutting board; tent with foil. Let stand for 10 minutes before slicing.

TIP For the best flavour, refrigerate the raw herbed roast overnight. Tightly cover with plastic wrap to keep all the wonderful (but strong) aromas in.

Makes 8 to 10 servings. PER EACH OF 10 SERVINGS: about 201 cal, 27 g pro, 9 g total fat (3 g sat. fat), 1 g carb, trace fibre, 66 mg chol, 191 mg sodium, 372 mg potassium. % RDI: 1% calcium, 6% iron, 2% vit A, 5% vit C, 2% folate.

Porchetta-Style Oven Pork Roast

Prepare roast as directed; place on rack in roasting pan. Pour in ½ cup water. Roast in 350°F (180°C) oven until juices run clear when pork is pierced and just a hint of pink remains inside, or instant-read thermometer inserted in centre reads 160°F (71°C), 1½ to 1¾ hours.

MOJO-GLAZED SPIRAL HAM

**This festive ham gives a nod to Cuban-style mojo sauce,
a vibrant blend of savoury spices and bright citrus flavours. Got leftovers?
They make the most delicious ham sandwiches on buttered pillowy bread.**

Stir together cumin, coriander, paprika, sugar and pepper; rub all over ham. Place ham, flat side down, on rack in roasting pan; pour in 1 cup water. Cover tightly with foil; roast in 325°F (160°C) oven until instant-read thermometer inserted in centre reads 130°F (55°C), about 2 hours.

MOJO GLAZE: Meanwhile, in saucepan, heat oil over medium heat; cook onion and garlic, stirring, until softened, about 4 minutes. Add cumin and coriander; cook, stirring, for 1 minute. Stir in orange juice and bring to boil; cook over medium-high heat until reduced to 1 cup, about 20 minutes. Brush half over ham.

Roast ham, covered and brushing with remaining glaze halfway through, until instant-read thermometer inserted in centre reads 140°F (60°C), about 1 hour.

Transfer ham to cutting board; tent with foil. Let stand for 20 minutes before serving.

1 tbsp each **ground cumin** and **ground coriander**

1 tbsp **sweet paprika**

1 tsp **granulated sugar**

½ tsp **pepper**

9 lb (4 kg) **fully cooked bone-in spiral-cut ham**

MOJO GLAZE:

2 tbsp **extra-virgin olive oil**

1 small **onion,** minced

4 cloves **garlic,** minced

1 tsp each **ground cumin** and **ground coriander**

2 cups **orange juice**

Makes 24 servings. PER SERVING: about 251 cal, 28 g pro, 13 g total fat (4 g sat. fat), 9 g carb, 1 g fibre, 85 mg chol, 1,653 mg sodium, 231 mg potassium. % RDI: 1% calcium, 24% iron, 2% vit A, 14% vit C, 3% folate.

WHOLE HAM GLAZED WITH RED WINE & QUATRE ÉPICES

Quatre épices, or four spices, is a mix used in French dishes. It consists of pepper, nutmeg, cloves and ginger, and pairs nicely with honey, red wine and Dijon mustard on a simple baked ham.

15 lb (6.75 kg) **fully cooked bone-in whole ham**

½ cup **liquid honey**

¼ cup **red wine** or pineapple juice

2 tbsp **butter**

1½ tsp **pepper**

1 tsp grated **nutmeg**

½ tsp each **ground cloves** and **ground ginger**

1 tbsp **Dijon mustard**

Whole cloves

Place ham, fat side up, on rack in roasting pan; pour in 2 cups water. Cover pan tightly with foil; roast in 325°F (160°C) oven for 2 hours, adding more water if necessary to maintain level.

If ham has skin, slide sharp knife under skin and lift off. Trim fat layer to ¼-inch (5 mm) thickness. Diagonally score fat to form diamond pattern.

In small saucepan, combine honey, wine, butter, pepper, nutmeg, cloves and ginger over medium heat, stirring occasionally, until butter is melted. Stir in mustard; let cool slightly. Brush enough of the glaze over ham to cover; stud centre of each diamond with clove.

Roast ham, uncovered and brushing several times with remaining glaze, until instant-read thermometer inserted in centre reads 140°F (60°C), 45 to 60 minutes.

Transfer ham to cutting board; tent with foil. Let stand for 15 minutes before carving.

To carve, cut ham down to bone into ¼-inch (5 mm) thick slices. With knife parallel to bone, cut off slices along bone. Turn remaining meaty portion face up; repeat carving.

For brunch or when serving a smaller group (6 to 8 people), choose a 2 lb (900 g) boneless ham; then halve the remaining ingredients and baking time.

Makes 24 servings. PER SERVING: about 252 cal, 35 g pro, 9 g total fat (3 g sat. fat), 8 g carb, trace fibre, 79 mg chol, 1,874 mg sodium. % RDI: 1% calcium, 10% iron, 1% vit A, 3% folate.

CILANTRO LAMB RACKS

Cilantro and dried coriander (the seeds of the same plant) have just the right herbal, citrusy notes to complement meaty, slightly gamey roast lamb. Racks are a bit pricey, so stock up when they are on sale.

Whisk together cilantro, oil, garlic, ginger, coriander, salt and pepper. Rub all over lamb; let stand for 10 minutes. *(Make-ahead: Cover and refrigerate for up to 8 hours.)*

Place lamb, fat side down, in small roasting pan; roast in 425°F (220°C) oven until instant-read thermometer inserted in centre reads 145°F (63°C) for medium-rare, about 20 minutes.

Transfer lamb to cutting board; tent with foil. Let stand for 10 minutes before slicing between bones.

¼ cup chopped **fresh cilantro**

2 tbsp **vegetable oil**

2 cloves **garlic,** minced

1 tbsp minced **fresh ginger**

1½ tsp **ground coriander**

½ tsp each **salt** and **pepper**

2 **racks of lamb** (about 1¾ lb/ 790 g total)

Makes 4 servings. PER SERVING: about 256 cal, 22 g pro, 18 g total fat (4 g sat. fat), 2 g carb, trace fibre, 71 mg chol, 354 mg sodium. % RDI: 2% calcium, 12% iron, 1% vit A, 2% vit C, 9% folate.

MUSTARD-BREADED LAMB RACKS WITH BRAISED WHITE BEANS

This is what rustic French cuisine is all about. Frenched bones look so elegant, and they're not that hard to scrape clean (see Tip, below) – but if the butcher will do it for you, it's a step you can save. Interlocking the frenched bones is called a guard of honour, because it looks like the crossed swords at a military ceremony.

2 **racks of lamb,** frenched (about
  1½ lb/675 g total)

¼ tsp each **salt** and **pepper**

2 tbsp **Dijon mustard**

1 large clove **garlic,** minced

2 tsp minced **fresh thyme**
  (or ½ tsp dried)

2 tbsp **extra-virgin olive oil**

¾ cup **fresh bread crumbs**

Braised White Beans (opposite)

Sprinkle lamb with salt and pepper. Whisk together mustard, garlic and thyme; spread over meaty side of racks. Let stand for 30 minutes.

Meanwhile, in skillet, heat oil over medium-high heat; cook bread crumbs, stirring, until crisp and golden, about 5 minutes. Let cool slightly. Press onto meaty side of racks.

With rib ends up, press racks together, interweaving bones. Pull bases about 1 inch (2.5 cm) apart to stabilize; place on baking sheet.

Roast lamb in 425°F (220°C) oven until instant-read thermometer inserted in centre reads 145°F (63°C) for medium-rare, about 25 minutes.

Transfer lamb to cutting board; let stand for 5 minutes before slicing between bones. Serve with beans.

Frenching a rack of lamb isn't hard; it's just a little time-consuming. Using a sharp carving knife, scrape clean the ends of each rib bone to within 1 inch (2.5 cm) of the eye of the raw meat.

Makes 4 servings. PER SERVING: about 633 cal, 30 g pro, 37 g total fat (13 g sat. fat), 44 g carb, 10 g fibre, 81 mg chol, 920 mg sodium. % RDI: 14% calcium, 37% iron, 40% vit A, 14% vit C, 91% folate.

BRAISED WHITE BEANS

Dried beans are a budget saver. Plus, when you cook them yourself, you control the amount of added sodium, which can be high in canned beans.

BEANS: Rinse beans; soak overnight in 3 cups water. (Or, for the quick-soak method, bring to boil and boil gently for 2 minutes. Remove from heat; cover and let stand for 1 hour. Drain.) Place soaked beans in saucepan with 3 times their volume of water. Add onion, bay leaf and thyme; bring to boil. Reduce heat, cover and simmer until beans are tender, 45 minutes. Drain; discard onion, bay leaf and thyme. *(Make-ahead: Refrigerate in airtight container for up to 24 hours.)*

In skillet, heat oil over medium heat; cook onions, celery, carrot, garlic, salt, thyme and pepper, stirring occasionally, until onions are softened and lightly browned, about 10 minutes.

Stir in wine, scraping up browned bits; cook until almost no liquid remains, about 30 seconds.

Add beans, tomatoes, broth and 1 cup water. Bring to boil; reduce heat and simmer until sauce coats beans and celery is tender, 25 to 30 minutes. Stir in butter. *(Make-ahead: Let cool for 30 minutes. Refrigerate in airtight container for up to 24 hours.)*

2 tbsp **extra-virgin olive oil**
2 small **onions,** diced
1 rib **celery,** diced
1 **carrot,** diced
2 cloves **garlic,** minced
½ tsp **salt**
¼ tsp minced **fresh thyme**
¼ tsp **pepper**
¼ cup **dry white wine** or water
1 cup chopped seeded peeled **tomatoes**
1 cup **vegetable broth**
1 tbsp **butter**

BEANS:
1 cup **dried navy beans**
1 **onion**
1 **bay leaf**
3 sprigs **fresh thyme**

Makes 4 servings. PER SERVING: about 293 cal, 11 g pro, 10 g total fat (3 g sat. fat), 40 g carb, 10 g fibre, 8 mg chol, 577 mg sodium. % RDI: 10% calcium, 24% iron, 40% vit A, 13% vit C, 81% folate.

GREMOLATA RACK OF LAMB

Gremolata is a traditional Milanese condiment for roasted or grilled meats. There are many variations, but all include lemon zest, garlic and parsley; in this recipe, we've added some ground coriander to the mix for a different type of citrusy note.

2 **racks of lamb,** frenched (about
2½ lb/1.125 kg total)
¼ tsp each **salt** and **pepper**

GREMOLATA:
½ cup minced **fresh parsley**
2 tbsp **extra-virgin olive oil**
4 tsp grated **lemon zest**
2 cloves **garlic,** minced
½ tsp **ground coriander**
¼ tsp each **salt** and **pepper**

GREMOLATA: Mix together parsley, oil, lemon zest, garlic, coriander, salt and pepper.

Trim any outside fat from lamb; sprinkle with salt and pepper. Press gremolata onto meaty side of racks. Place lamb, gremolata side up, in roasting pan.

Roast lamb in 450°F (230°C) oven for 10 minutes. Reduce heat to 325°F (160°C); roast until instant-read thermometer inserted in centre reads 145°F (63°C) for medium-rare, about 15 minutes. (Or grill lamb, covered, over medium heat until medium-rare, about 20 minutes total.)

Transfer lamb to cutting board; tent with foil. Let stand for 5 minutes before slicing between bones.

Makes 4 servings. PER SERVING: about 253 cal, 24 g pro, 16 g total fat (5 g sat. fat), 2 g carb, 1 g fibre, 89 mg chol, 337 mg sodium. % RDI: 3% calcium, 17% iron, 4% vit A, 20% vit C, 5% folate.

ROSEMARY RACK OF LAMB FOR TWO

**This gorgeous little rosemary-scented rack of lamb is the perfect romantic dinner.
Serve with your favourite sides and a nice bottle of red wine to complement the tender meat.**

Combine bread crumbs, rosemary, Parmesan cheese, garlic, salt and pepper. Spread mustard evenly over lamb; coat with bread crumb mixture.

In ovenproof skillet, heat oil over medium-high heat; cook lamb, fat side down, until golden, about 2 minutes.

Roast lamb in 425°F (220°C) oven until instant-read thermometer inserted in centre reads 145°F (63°C) for medium-rare, about 15 minutes.

Transfer lamb to cutting board; tent with foil. Let stand for 5 minutes before slicing between bones.

¼ cup **fresh bread crumbs**
1 tbsp chopped **fresh rosemary**
1 tbsp grated **Parmesan cheese**
1 clove **garlic,** minced
Pinch each **salt** and **pepper**
1 tbsp **Dijon mustard**
1 **rack of lamb** (1 lb/450 g)
1 tbsp **extra-virgin olive oil**

TIP If you find the taste of lamb too gamey, give local lamb a try. Imported lamb, often from New Zealand, is a common sight in grocery stores – it's high quality and a good value but has a stronger flavour than locally raised varieties.

Makes 2 servings. PER SERVING: about 316 cal, 27 g pro, 21 g total fat (6 g sat. fat), 4 g carb, 1 g fibre, 86 mg chol, 254 mg sodium. % RDI: 7% calcium, 15% iron, 1% vit A, 2% vit C, 12% folate.

ROAST LEG OF LAMB WITH RED WINE JUS

Mixing the pan drippings from this succulent roast with red wine makes a rich, savoury jus (which means "juice" in French) to spoon over tender slices of the meat. Cooking the roast on the bone yields more flavour and makes a spectacular presentation for carving.

3 lb (1.35 kg) **bone-in leg of lamb**

2 cloves **garlic,** slivered

1½ tsp **salt**

1 tsp **dried Italian herb seasoning**

½ tsp **coarsely ground pepper**

2 tbsp **olive oil**

1½ cups **sodium-reduced beef broth** (approx)

1 cup **red wine**

2 tsp **cornstarch**

Trim fat from lamb. Cut slits all over lamb; insert garlic sliver in each. Rub all over with salt, Italian herb seasoning and pepper; drizzle with 1 tbsp of the oil. Place on rack in small roasting pan.

Roast lamb in 400°F (200°C) oven for 30 minutes. Reduce heat to 325°F (160°C). Whisk 1 cup of the broth with remaining oil; pour over lamb. Roast, basting with pan juices every 15 minutes and adding more broth if necessary, until instant-read thermometer inserted in centre reads 145°F (63°C) for medium-rare, about 1¼ hours.

Transfer lamb to cutting board; tent with foil. Let stand for 15 minutes before carving (see Tip, below).

Place pan over medium heat; add wine and remaining broth to pan juices; bring to boil. Whisk cornstarch with 2 tbsp water and stir into pan; simmer until thickened. Strain and serve with lamb.

TIP

To carve a bone-in leg of lamb, place on cutting board, meatier side up. Grip shank end firmly with towel. Cutting down to bone, cut ¼-inch (5 mm) thick slices. Then, with knife parallel to bone, cut slices from bone. Turn lamb, remaining meatier side up. Carve as for first side.

Makes 6 servings. PER SERVING: about 288 cal, 33 g pro, 14 g total fat (5 g sat. fat), 2 g carb, trace fibre, 77 mg chol, 239 mg sodium, 453 mg potassium. % RDI: 4% calcium, 16% iron, 9% folate.

MEXICAN SLOW-ROASTED LEG OF LAMB

Slow roasting produces exceptionally tender lamb and allows the Mexican herbs and spices to permeate the meat. You can substitute 2 tsp ancho chili powder for the whole ancho pepper; just mix it in with the ground spices.

5 lb (2.25 kg) **bone-in leg of lamb**

1 **white onion,** cut in 1-inch (2.5 cm) thick slices

1 **ancho pepper**

2 **bay leaves**

Half stick **Mexican cinnamon** or regular cinnamon

12 **black peppercorns**

5 **whole cloves**

5 cloves **garlic**

1½ tsp **dried oregano**

1¼ tsp **salt**

¼ cup **orange juice**

5 tsp **cider vinegar**

1 tbsp **chili powder**

Trim most of the fat from lamb, leaving thin layer on top. With thin sharp knife, poke about twelve 2-inch (5 cm) deep slits into top.

In small (preferably cast-iron) skillet, cook onion over medium heat, turning once, until tender and lightly charred. Remove and set aside.

Add ancho pepper to pan; toast on both sides until fragrant and slightly darkened. Remove seeds; break pepper into small pieces; set aside.

Add bay leaves to pan; toast until dry and fragrant. Remove from pan and set aside. Add cinnamon, peppercorns and cloves to pan; toast until fragrant and slightly darkened. Break up cinnamon stick. In spice grinder, grind together toasted ancho pepper, bay leaves, cinnamon, peppercorns and cloves until finely powdered.

In food processor, purée together onion, garlic, oregano and salt. Transfer to bowl; stir in spice mixture, orange juice, vinegar and chili powder.

Place lamb in roasting pan; rub all over with spice mixture. Cover with foil. Roast in 400°F (200°C) oven for 20 minutes. Reduce heat to 275°F (140°C); cover and roast for 3 hours.

Baste with pan juices; uncover and roast, basting every 30 minutes, until fork-tender, about 2 hours. Let stand for 10 minutes before carving (see Tip, page 196).

Makes 6 servings. PER SERVING: about 405 cal, 55 g pro, 17 g total fat (7 g sat. fat), 9 g carb, 2 g fibre, 128 mg chol, 638 mg sodium, 870 mg potassium. % RDI: 8% calcium, 30% iron, 11% vit A, 13% vit C, 22% folate.

MUSTARD PAPRIKA BUTTERFLIED LEG OF LAMB

A lovely amber crust surrounds this juicy lamb, which you can grill or roast depending on the season. If you aren't keen on using wine in the marinade, use 4 tsp each wine vinegar and water instead. Buying an already-butterflied leg of lamb is the easiest option, but follow the tip (below) if you want to do it yourself.

MARINADE: In large bowl, whisk together wine, mustard, oil, paprika, salt, pepper and cayenne pepper; add lamb, turning to coat. Cover and refrigerate for 2 hours. *(Make-ahead: Refrigerate for up to 12 hours.)*

Grill lamb, covered, on greased grill over medium heat for 15 minutes. Turn and grill until instant-read thermometer inserted in centre reads 145°F (63°C) for medium-rare, about 30 minutes. (Or roast in 325°F/160°C oven until instant-read thermometer inserted in centre reads 145°F (63°C) for medium-rare, about 1 hour.)

Transfer lamb to cutting board; tent with foil. Let stand for 5 minutes before thinly slicing across the grain.

2½ lb (1.125 kg) **boneless leg of lamb,** butterflied

MARINADE:
3 tbsp **white wine**
2 tbsp **Dijon mustard**
1 tbsp **vegetable oil**
2 tsp **sweet paprika**
¾ tsp each **salt** and **pepper**
¼ tsp **cayenne pepper**

TIP

To butterfly a leg of lamb, on cutting board and using boning or paring knife, trim fat from lamb, leaving membrane. Starting at wide end close to bone and using short strokes with tip of knife, cut around flat pelvic bone to loosen. Holding pelvic bone, cut through tendons of ball-and-socket joint connecting pelvic bone to thigh bone. Turn lamb fat side up. Cutting right to thigh bone, cut leg open lengthwise. Following close to bone and using short strokes, cut meat and tendons away from bone to ball-and-socket joint connected to shank bone. Cut meat away from shank bone; discard bones or save for stock. Lay meat membrane side down. From inside edge of one of two thickest lobes of meat, holding knife blade flat, cut in half horizontally almost but not all the way through; repeat on opposite lobe. Open like book to form as even thickness as possible.

Makes 6 servings. PER SERVING: about 220 cal, 33 g pro, 9 g total fat (3 g sat. fat), 1 g carb, trace fibre, 117 mg chol, 407 mg sodium. % RDI: 2% calcium, 21% iron, 5% vit A, 2% vit C.

ROAST LEG OF LAMB WITH CARAMELIZED ONION GRAVY

This leg of lamb is an impressive centrepiece for any celebratory table. The browned bits scraped up from the bottom of the roasting pan add a huge amount of umami (savoury) goodness to the gravy.

6 lb (2.7 kg) **bone-in leg of lamb**

2 cloves **garlic,** thinly sliced lengthwise

2 **sprigs fresh rosemary**

¼ tsp each **salt** and **pepper**

CARAMELIZED ONION GRAVY:

2 tsp **olive oil**

2 cloves **garlic,** minced

1 **onion,** thinly sliced

¼ cup **red wine**

2 cups **sodium-reduced beef broth**

¼ tsp **pepper**

1 tsp **cornstarch**

Trim most of the fat from lamb, leaving thin layer on top. With thin sharp knife, poke about twelve 1½-inch (4 cm) deep slits into top. Stuff each slit with 1 slice garlic. Remove leaves from rosemary sprigs; stuff 4 or 5 leaves into each slit. Cover and refrigerate for 1 hour. *(Make-ahead: Refrigerate for up to 24 hours.)* Sprinkle with salt and pepper.

Place lamb on greased rack in roasting pan; roast in 350°F (180°C) oven until instant-read thermometer inserted in centre reads 145°F (63°C) for medium-rare, about 2 hours.

Transfer lamb to cutting board; tent with foil. Let stand for 15 minutes before carving (see Tip, page 196).

CARAMELIZED ONION GRAVY:
Meanwhile, in saucepan, heat oil over medium heat; cook garlic, stirring, for 1 minute. Add onion; cook, stirring occasionally, until golden, about 8 minutes. Stir in wine; cook, stirring, for 1 minute. Add broth and pepper; bring to boil. Remove from heat.

Drain fat from roasting pan; place pan over medium-high heat. Add onion mixture and bring to boil, scraping up browned bits. Stir cornstarch with ¼ cup water; whisk into pan. Cook, stirring, until slightly thickened, about 3 minutes. Serve with lamb.

Makes 12 servings. PER SERVING: about 274 cal, 39 g pro, 11 g total fat (5 g sat. fat), 2 g carb, trace fibre, 129 mg chol, 271 mg sodium, 654 mg potassium. % RDI: 2% calcium, 18% iron, 1% vit A, 2% vit C, 10% folate.

GARLIC & BACON-STUFFED LEG OF LAMB WITH ROSEMARY

Rosemary, garlic and lamb are a heavenly trio, and offer a perfect welcome to spring. Serve this special roast with Buttermilk Smashed Potatoes (page 185) and tender, young asparagus.

4 lb (1.8 kg) **short cut leg of lamb**

6 cloves **garlic,** slivered

2 slices **bacon,** chopped

2 tbsp **extra-virgin olive oil**

1 tbsp chopped **fresh rosemary** (or 1 tsp dried)

1 tsp **sea salt** or table salt

1 tsp **cracked black pepper**

Using sharp knife, remove thin membrane from lamb. Cut slits all over lamb; insert garlic sliver and bacon into each. Brush oil over lamb. Sprinkle with rosemary, salt and pepper.

Place lamb on greased rack in roasting pan; roast in 325°F (160°C) oven until instant-read thermometer inserted in centre reads 145°F (63°C) for medium-rare, about 1 hour and 40 minutes.

Transfer lamb to cutting board; tent with foil. Let stand for 15 minutes before carving (see Tip, page 196).

Meanwhile, skim fat off pan drippings; place pan over medium-high heat. Add ½ cup water; bring to boil, scraping up browned bits. Strain and serve with lamb.

TIP

A short cut leg of lamb is about three-quarters of a whole leg – the sirloin portion at the top of the leg has been removed. It's a nice amount of meat for a party. Because it's shorter, it's also an easier size to cook in the oven or on the barbecue.

Makes 6 servings. PER SERVING: about 445 cal, 43 g pro, 29 g total fat (11 g sat. fat), 1 g carb, trace fibre, 139 mg chol, 523 mg sodium. % RDI: 2% calcium, 28% iron, 2% vit C, 14% folate.

ROAST LEG OF LAMB WITH 40 CLOVES OF GARLIC

Forty cloves sure seems like a lot of garlic – but it comes out so sweet and caramelized that you'll be asking for more. Anchovies add a pleasant saltiness to the meat, but no fishiness, so don't avoid them even if you're not normally a fan.

In small saucepan, bring garlic, broth and 1 cup water to boil; reduce heat and simmer for 10 minutes. Remove 3 cloves; cut into about 24 slivers.

Meanwhile, soak anchovies in water for 5 minutes; drain and pat dry. Cut into 24 pieces and set aside.

Using sharp knife, remove thin membrane from lamb. Cut 24 tiny slits all over lamb; insert 1 garlic sliver and 1 anchovy piece in each.

Combine oil, rosemary and thyme; brush all over lamb. Sprinkle with salt and pepper.

Place lamb on greased rack in roasting pan; pour in broth mixture and whole garlic cloves. Roast in 325°F (160°C) oven, basting often with broth, until instant-read thermometer inserted in centre reads 145°F (63°C) for medium-rare, about 1 hour and 40 minutes.

Transfer lamb to cutting board; tent with foil. Let stand for 15 minutes before carving (see Tip, page 196).

Skim fat off pan juices; spoon juices and garlic over lamb.

40 cloves **garlic,** peeled (about 3 large heads)

1 cup **sodium-reduced beef broth**

3 **anchovy fillets**

4 lb (1.8 kg) **short cut leg of lamb**

2 tbsp **extra-virgin olive oil**

1 tbsp minced **fresh rosemary**

1 tsp **dried thyme**

¼ tsp **sea salt** or table salt

¼ tsp **pepper**

Makes 6 servings. PER SERVING: about 381 cal, 43 g pro, 19 g total fat (5 g sat. fat), 7 g carb, 1 g fibre, 127 mg chol, 397 mg sodium. % RDI: 5% calcium, 31% iron, 8% vit C, 14% folate.

BRAISING CUTS

RECIPES

OVEN-BRAISED BARBECUE BRISKET

Flavourful spices make this tender roast a winner. For an informal family get-together, thinly slice and serve on kaiser rolls for tasty barbecue sandwiches. If you can't find strained tomatoes, just process 1 can (28 oz/796 mL) whole tomatoes in the blender until smooth and strain out the seeds.

3 tbsp **sweet paprika**

1 tbsp **kosher salt**

1 tbsp **pepper**

1 tbsp **granulated sugar**

1 tbsp **ancho chili powder** (or chili powder plus ¼ tsp cayenne pepper)

2 tsp **garlic powder**

3 tbsp **vegetable oil**

4 lb (1.8 kg) **double beef brisket pot roast**

BARBECUE SAUCE:

1 **onion,** coarsely chopped

4 cloves **garlic**

1 bottle (660 mL) **strained tomatoes** (passata)

½ cup packed **brown sugar**

⅓ cup **cider vinegar**

2 tbsp **Worcestershire sauce**

1 bottle (341 mL) **beer**

In large bowl, combine paprika, salt, pepper, sugar, chili powder and garlic powder; stir in oil to make paste.

Add brisket, turning and rubbing paste in well. Cover and let stand for 1 hour. *(Make-ahead: Refrigerate for up to 24 hours.)*

Place brisket, fat side up, in greased roasting pan; roast in 400°F (200°C) oven for 30 minutes.

BARBECUE SAUCE: Meanwhile, in blender, mince onion with garlic. Add tomatoes, brown sugar, vinegar and Worcestershire sauce; whirl until no large chunks remain. Stir in beer. Pour over brisket.

Cover and braise in 325°F (160°C) oven, basting occasionally, for 2 hours. Uncover and braise until meat is tender, about 1 hour.

Transfer brisket to cutting board; tent with foil. Let stand for 10 minutes before thinly slicing across the grain. Serve with sauce.

Makes 8 to 10 servings. PER EACH OF 10 SERVINGS: about 413 cal, 40 g pro, 18 g total fat (5 g sat. fat), 23 g carb, 3 g fibre, 85 mg chol, 671 mg sodium. % RDI: 5% calcium, 40% iron, 16% vit A, 13% vit C, 9% folate.

SLOW COOKER WINE-BRAISED BRISKET

Red wine infuses this fork-tender meat, while soy sauce and cranberry juice add a nice balance of saltiness and sweetness. For this pot roast, you can use either a double brisket or a regular brisket. You may need to cut a larger one in half to fit it into the slow cooker.

In large bowl, combine salt, pepper, rosemary and cayenne pepper; rub about half over brisket. Toss onions with remainder. Arrange brisket, fat side up, on onions in bowl.

Stir together wine, broth, cranberry concentrate, soy sauce and garlic; pour over brisket. Cover and refrigerate for 12 hours. *(Make-ahead: Refrigerate for up to 24 hours.)*

Transfer onions and liquid to slow cooker; top with brisket. Cover and cook on low until meat is fall-apart tender, 5 to 6 hours.

Transfer brisket to cutting board; tent with foil. Let stand for 20 minutes before slicing across the grain.

Meanwhile, skim fat from liquid in slow cooker. Whisk flour with ⅓ cup water; whisk into liquid.

Cover and cook on high until thickened, about 20 minutes. Serve with brisket. *(Make-ahead: Let brisket and sauce cool separately for 30 minutes. Combine brisket and sauce in uncovered airtight container; refrigerate until cold. Cover and refrigerate for up to 2 days or freeze for up to 1 month.)*

1¼ tsp **salt**

¾ tsp **pepper**

¾ tsp crumbled **dried rosemary**

¼ tsp **cayenne pepper**

4 lb (1.8 kg) **double beef brisket pot roast**

2 large **onions,** sliced

¾ cup **dry red wine**

½ cup **beef broth**

½ cup thawed **cranberry cocktail concentrate**

¼ cup **soy sauce**

4 large cloves **garlic,** minced

¼ cup **all-purpose flour**

TIP

A whole brisket is made up of two muscles: the triangular flat and the point (the raised muscle at one end of the flat). You can buy a whole brisket, just the point, just the flat or a double brisket, which includes the point and part of the flat. A double brisket conveniently contains both lean and juicier, fattier meat all in one roast.

Makes 10 servings. PER SERVING: about 306 cal, 29 g pro, 15 g total fat (6 g sat. fat), 13 g carb, 1 g fibre, 73 mg chol, 805 mg sodium. % RDI: 2% calcium, 23% iron, 17% vit C, 7% folate.

ROSEMARY-RUBBED BEEF BRISKET

Mustard, rosemary and red wine give this brisket an earthy but bright flavour that's just as good for entertaining as it is for a simple Sunday dinner with family. Serve with mashed or boiled potatoes and your favourite steamed green vegetable.

6 cloves **garlic,** minced

3 tbsp minced **fresh rosemary**

3 tbsp **extra-virgin olive oil**

2 tbsp **Dijon mustard**

½ tsp **onion powder**

½ tsp **pepper**

4 lb (1.8 kg) **double beef brisket pot roast**

¼ tsp **kosher salt** or table salt

2 cups **dry red wine**

2 cups **sodium-reduced beef broth**

2 tbsp **cornstarch**

Stir together garlic, rosemary, 2 tbsp of the oil, the mustard, onion powder and pepper; rub all over brisket. Cover and refrigerate for 2 hours. *(Make-ahead: Refrigerate for up to 24 hours.)*

Sprinkle brisket with salt. In large skillet, heat remaining oil over medium-high heat; brown brisket all over. Transfer to large roasting pan.

Stir wine with broth; pour into pan. Cover and braise in 325°F (160°C) oven until fork-tender, 3 to 4 hours. Transfer brisket to cutting board; tent with foil. Let stand for 10 minutes before thinly slicing across the grain.

Meanwhile, strain pan juices through fine sieve; skim off fat. Return juices to pan and bring to boil. Whisk cornstarch with 2 tbsp water; whisk into pan. Cook, whisking, until slightly thickened, about 1 minute. Serve with brisket. *(Make-ahead: Let brisket and sauce cool separately for 30 minutes. Return brisket to sauce; cover and refrigerate for up to 24 hours. Thinly slice brisket across the grain; arrange in sauce. Cover and reheat in 325°F/ 160°C oven until hot, about 1 hour.)*

Makes 10 to 12 servings. PER EACH OF 12 SERVINGS: about 381 cal, 28 g pro, 28 g total fat (10 g sat. fat), 3 g carb, trace fibre, 97 mg chol, 271 mg sodium, 470 mg potassium. % RDI: 2% calcium, 20% iron, 3% folate.

SLOW COOKER MUSHROOM POT ROAST

This tender, old-school pot roast – and its luscious gravy – captures the essence of fall cooking. Mushroom lovers will be thrilled to come home to it after a busy day at work, school or play.

3 lb (1.35 kg) **boneless beef cross rib pot roast**

½ tsp each **salt** and **pepper**

2 tbsp **vegetable oil** (approx)

1 **onion,** diced

2 each **carrots** and ribs **celery,** sliced

3 cloves **garlic,** minced

1 tsp each **dried marjoram** and **dried oregano**

4 cups **button mushrooms,** quartered

⅓ cup **sodium-reduced beef broth**

2 tbsp **tomato paste**

2 tsp **Worcestershire sauce**

3 tbsp **all-purpose flour**

Sprinkle roast with salt and pepper. In large skillet, heat half of the oil over medium-high heat; brown roast all over, adding more oil if necessary. Transfer to slow cooker.

Drain any fat from pan; add remaining oil. Cook onion, carrots, celery, garlic, marjoram and oregano over medium heat until softened, about 5 minutes. Add mushrooms; cook until tender, 5 minutes. Scrape into slow cooker.

Stir broth into pan, scraping up browned bits; boil for 1 minute. Add to slow cooker along with tomato paste and Worcestershire sauce; cover and cook on low until roast is tender, 5 to 7 hours.

Transfer roast to cutting board; tent with foil. Let stand for 15 minutes before thinly slicing across the grain.

Meanwhile, whisk flour with ¼ cup water; whisk into slow cooker. Cover and cook on high until thickened, about 15 minutes. Serve with beef.

Makes 4 to 6 servings. PER EACH OF 6 SERVINGS: about 454 cal, 47 g pro, 23 g total fat (8 g sat. fat), 11 g carb, 2 g fibre, 114 mg chol, 347 mg sodium. % RDI: 4% calcium, 42% iron, 44% vit A, 8% vit C, 15% folate.

BRAISED ROLLED FLANK STEAK

**Flank steak is pretty mild on its own, but the salami-olive stuffing is bursting with flavour.
Bring the whole rolled, stuffed steak to the table and carve it in front of guests for a gorgeous presentation.**

STUFFING: In bowl, beat egg. Toss in bread crumbs, salami, garlic, olives, parsley and capers.

Starting at long side of steak and holding knife parallel to cutting board, make horizontal cuts, cutting steak in half almost but not all the way through; open like book.

Leaving ½-inch (1 cm) border on all sides, spread stuffing over steak. Starting at 1 side, roll up steak; tie at 1½-inch (4 cm) intervals with kitchen string.

In large Dutch oven, heat oil over medium-high heat; brown steak all over. Transfer to plate.

Drain fat from pan; cook onion, garlic, marjoram, thyme, salt and pepper, stirring occasionally, until softened, about 5 minutes. Add wine; bring to boil. Mash in tomatoes. Add tomato paste and return to boil; reduce heat and simmer for 10 minutes.

Return steak and any accumulated juices to pan; spoon sauce over top. Cover and braise in 300°F (150°C) oven, turning and spooning sauce over top halfway through, until tender, about 2 hours.

Transfer steak to cutting board; tent with foil. Let stand for 5 minutes before cutting into 12 slices.

Meanwhile, bring sauce to boil; reduce heat and simmer until sauce flows slowly when spatula is drawn across bottom of pot, about 5 minutes. Serve with steak.

2 lb (900 g) **beef flank marinating steak**
1 tbsp **vegetable oil**
1 **onion,** chopped
2 cloves **garlic,** minced
1 tsp **dried marjoram**
½ tsp **dried thyme**
¼ tsp each **salt** and **pepper**
¼ cup **red wine**
1 can (28 oz/796 mL) **whole tomatoes**
2 tbsp **tomato paste**

STUFFING:
1 **egg**
1 cup **fresh bread crumbs**
½ cup finely chopped **salami** or ham
2 cloves **garlic,** minced
¼ cup chopped rinsed **green olives**
¼ cup chopped **fresh parsley**
1 tbsp rinsed drained **capers**

Makes 6 servings. PER SERVING: about 370 cal, 39 g pro, 17 g total fat (6 g sat. fat), 14 g carb, 2 g fibre, 100 mg chol, 756 mg sodium. % RDI: 7% calcium, 33% iron, 12% vit A, 42% vit C, 15% folate.

RED WINE GARLIC POT ROAST

With pretty pearl onions, fresh shiitake mushrooms and rich red wine, this tender stewed roast has a special flair that makes it perfect for entertaining. To peel the pearl onions easily, blanch them in a large pot of boiling water for 1 minute; drain and plunge into cold water, then drain and peel.

In heatproof bowl, pour boiling water over dried mushrooms; let stand until softened, about 20 minutes. Reserving liquid, strain mushrooms. Discard stems. Slice caps; set aside.

Sprinkle roast with salt and pepper. In large Dutch oven, heat 1 tbsp of the oil over medium-high heat; brown roast all over. Transfer to plate.

Add remaining oil to pan; cook diced onions and garlic over medium heat, stirring occasionally, until softened, 3 to 4 minutes. Add fresh mushrooms, soaked mushrooms, bay leaf and allspice; cook for 2 minutes. Add tomato paste; cook for 1 minute.

Add wine, broth and reserved mushroom liquid, scraping up any browned bits. Return roast and any accumulated juices to pan; bring to boil. Remove from heat.

Cover and braise in 300°F (150°C) oven, basting every 30 minutes and turning once, for 2½ hours.

Meanwhile, in skillet, melt butter over medium heat; cook pearl onions until tender and golden, about 10 minutes. Add to roast; cook, uncovered, until fork-tender, about 30 minutes. Discard bay leaf.

Transfer roast to cutting board; tent with foil. Let stand for 15 minutes before slicing across the grain. Serve sauce and onions with beef.

1 cup **boiling water**

1 pkg (14 g) **dried shiitake mushrooms**

3 lb (1.35 kg) **boneless beef blade pot roast**

½ tsp each **salt** and **pepper**

3 tbsp **vegetable oil**

2 **onions,** diced

10 cloves **garlic,** sliced

2 cups **fresh shiitake mushrooms,** stemmed and quartered (about 4 oz/115 g total)

1 **bay leaf**

Pinch **ground allspice**

2 tbsp **tomato paste**

1 cup each **red wine** and **sodium-reduced beef broth**

1 tbsp **butter**

1 pkg (10 oz/284 g) **pearl onions,** peeled

Makes 8 to 10 servings. PER EACH OF 10 SERVINGS: about 329 cal, 28 g pro, 20 g total fat (6 g sat. fat), 8 g carb, 1 g fibre, 83 mg chol, 283 mg sodium, 395 mg potassium. % RDI: 3% calcium, 22% iron, 2% vit A, 5% vit C, 7% folate.

BRAISED BRISKET WITH ONIONS

Brisket is easiest to carve once it's cooled. To make it ahead, cook, then cool and refrigerate the whole brisket and vegetables separately. Before reheating, slice the brisket across the grain. Combine brisket and vegetables in roasting pan, cover and heat in 325°F (160°C) oven for about 30 minutes.

3 lb (1.35 kg) **single beef brisket pot roast with fat cap attached**

3 large **onions,** sliced

6 **carrots,** cut in 2-inch (5 cm) pieces

RUB:
2 tbsp **vegetable oil**

2 cloves **garlic,** minced

1 tbsp **sweet paprika**

2 tsp **kosher salt** or salt

1 tsp **dry mustard**

½ tsp **pepper**

RUB: Stir together oil, garlic, paprika, salt, mustard and pepper. Rub all over brisket. Place in large roasting pan; cover and refrigerate for 2 hours. *(Make-ahead: Refrigerate for up to 24 hours.)*

Arrange onions and carrots in pan under brisket. Pour 1 cup water into pan. Cover and roast in 325°F (160°C) oven for 2 hours.

Add ½ cup water; roast until brisket is fork-tender, 1½ to 2 hours.

Transfer brisket to cutting board; tent with foil. Let stand for 15 minutes before slicing across the grain. Drizzle pan juices over brisket; serve with onions and carrots.

Makes 6 to 8 servings. PER EACH OF 8 SERVINGS: about 435 cal, 31 g pro, 29 g total fat (10 g sat. fat), 11 g carb, 3 g fibre, 107 mg chol, 535 mg sodium, 705 mg potassium. % RDI: 4% calcium, 24% iron, 100% vit A, 5% vit C, 11% folate.

CLASSIC SCALLOPED POTATOES

Who doesn't love scalloped potatoes any day of the week? This lightened-up take on the quintessential side dish boasts a hint of garlic and is made with 2% milk. It tastes just as good as the heavier cream-based version with any sort of meaty dish.

In saucepan, melt butter over medium heat; cook garlic, stirring, for 1 minute. Add flour, thyme, salt and pepper; cook, stirring, for 1 minute.

Gradually whisk in milk; cook, whisking constantly, until boiling and thickened, about 8 minutes.

Peel and thinly slice potatoes. Layer one-third in greased 8-inch (2 L) square baking dish or casserole dish; spread half of the onion over top. Repeat layers. Arrange remaining potatoes over top. Pour sauce over top, using back of knife to ease sauce between layers.

Cover and bake in 350°F (180°C) oven for 1 hour. Uncover and bake until lightly browned and potatoes are tender, about 30 minutes. Let stand for 5 minutes before serving.

¼ cup **butter**
3 cloves **garlic,** minced
¼ cup **all-purpose flour**
1 tsp chopped **fresh thyme**
¾ tsp **salt**
½ tsp **pepper**
2½ cups **milk**
6 **yellow-fleshed potatoes** (about 2 lb/900 g total)
1 small **onion,** sliced

TIP To slice potatoes easily, cut a little piece off the bottom of each spud to stabilize it on the cutting board.

Makes 8 servings. PER SERVING: about 187 cal, 5 g pro, 7 g total fat (5 g sat. fat), 26 g carb, 2 g fibre, 21 mg chol, 292 mg sodium, 437 mg potassium. % RDI: 9% calcium, 4% iron, 9% vit A, 12% vit C, 9% folate.

SLOW COOKER SHORT RIBS

A little bacon goes a long way, and a little prep yields tender meat that practically cooks itself. Broiling short ribs before braising them cuts down the amount of fat in the final dish and gives the ribs a caramel note.

3 lb (1.35 kg) **beef simmering short ribs**

½ tsp each **salt** and **pepper**

3 thick slices **bacon,** chopped

1 **onion,** chopped

3 cloves **garlic,** minced

1 large **carrot,** diced

2 tsp **dried thyme**

½ cup **dry sherry** or sodium-reduced beef broth

½ cup **sodium-reduced beef broth**

2 tbsp **tomato paste**

2 tbsp **all-purpose flour**

1 **green onion,** sliced

Cut beef into 1-rib pieces, trimming off fat. Season with ¼ tsp each of the salt and pepper. Arrange on foil-lined baking sheet; broil, turning once, until well browned, 8 to 10 minutes. Transfer to slow cooker.

In large skillet, cook bacon over medium heat until crisp. Drain on paper towel–lined plate.

Drain fat from skillet; cook onion, garlic, carrot, thyme and remaining salt and pepper over medium heat, stirring occasionally, until onion is softened, about 5 minutes. Add to slow cooker along with bacon.

In skillet, whisk together sherry, broth and tomato paste; bring to boil, scraping up browned bits. Stir into slow cooker. Cover and cook on low until ribs are tender, 5 to 6 hours. Using slotted spoon, transfer ribs to serving dish; keep warm.

Skim fat from liquid in slow cooker. Whisk flour with ¼ cup water; whisk into liquid. Cover and cook on high until thickened, 8 to 10 minutes. Pour over ribs. Sprinkle with green onion.

Makes 4 to 6 servings. PER EACH OF 6 SERVINGS: about 335 cal, 22 g pro, 23 g total fat (10 g sat. fat), 10 g carb, 1 g fibre, 63 mg chol, 423 mg sodium, 561 mg potassium. % RDI: 3% calcium, 18% iron, 28% vit A, 5% vit C, 8% folate.

BALSAMIC-BRAISED BEEF RIBS

Balsamic vinegar has a pleasant acidity that cuts through the richness of this crowd-pleaser. English-cut beef ribs are meaty single portions that you can order at the butcher counter. Pair them with Roasted Accordion New Potatoes (page 227) for a satisfying supper.

Sprinkle ribs with pinch each of the salt and pepper. In large Dutch oven, heat oil over medium-high heat; brown ribs, in batches. Transfer to plate.

Drain all but 1 tbsp fat from pan; cook onion, garlic and rosemary, stirring, until onion is softened, about 4 minutes. Stir in tomato paste; cook for 1 minute. Add vinegar; cook, stirring, until slightly thickened, about 1 minute. Stir in broth, 1 cup water, bay leaves and remaining salt and pepper.

Return ribs to pan; cover and braise in 325°F (160°C) oven until meat is tender, 2 hours. With slotted spoon, transfer ribs to plate. Keep warm.

Skim fat from sauce; heat sauce, uncovered, over medium-high heat until thick enough to coat spoon, about 8 minutes. Discard bay leaves. Return ribs to pan, tossing to coat. Sprinkle with parsley.

6 pieces (3 inches/8 cm) **English-cut beef ribs** (about 4½ lb/2.025 kg)

¼ tsp each **salt** and **pepper**

1 tsp **vegetable oil**

1 large **onion,** thinly sliced

3 cloves **garlic,** minced

2 tsp chopped **fresh rosemary**

¼ cup **tomato paste**

¼ cup **balsamic vinegar**

1 cup **sodium-reduced beef broth**

3 **bay leaves**

¼ cup chopped **fresh parsley**

Makes 6 servings. PER SERVING: about 670 cal, 38 g pro, 53 g total fat (21 g sat. fat), 7 g carb, 1 g fibre, 123 mg chol, 338 mg sodium, 844 mg potassium. % RDI: 4% calcium, 24% iron, 4% vit A, 10% vit C, 8% folate.

SLOW COOKER GUINNESS-BRAISED SHORT RIBS

Guinness is the ideal rich stout for braising and tenderizing decadent short ribs. Leftovers make a fantastic sandwich: Shred the meat for the filling and pass the leftover sauce as a dip.

2 **onions,** thinly sliced

2 **carrots,** diced

1 rib **celery,** diced

3 cloves **garlic,** minced

2 **bay leaves**

2 tsp **smoked paprika**

1¼ tsp **salt**

½ tsp **pepper**

2 cups **sodium-reduced beef broth**

1 can (440 mL) **Guinness beer**

¼ cup **tomato paste**

1 tbsp each **Dijon mustard** and **liquid honey**

3 lb (1.35 kg) **beef simmering short ribs,** trimmed

3 tbsp **all-purpose flour**

In slow cooker, combine onions, carrots, celery, garlic, bay leaves, paprika, salt and pepper. Whisk together broth, beer, tomato paste, mustard and honey; pour into slow cooker. Submerge ribs in liquid.

Cover and cook on low until meat is tender enough to pull away from bones, 7 to 8 hours.

Discard bay leaves. With slotted spoon, transfer ribs to plate; keep warm. Skim off fat from liquid in slow cooker.

Whisk flour with ¼ cup water until smooth; whisk into slow cooker. Cover and cook on high until slightly thickened, about 20 minutes.

Return ribs to sauce; stir to coat.

Makes 8 servings. PER SERVING: about 367 cal, 19 g pro, 27 g total fat (12 g sat. fat), 13 g carb, 2 g fibre, 58 mg chol, 616 mg sodium, 524 mg potassium. % RDI: 3% calcium, 14% iron, 36% vit A, 7% vit C, 10% folate.

BEEF & CABBAGE BORSCHT

Comfort food doesn't get much better than this eastern European stewy soup. Serve steaming bowls of it with crusty bread – or chewy bagels or bialys – for a wonderful cold-weather warm-up.

2 lb (900 g) **beef simmering short ribs**

1 **beef marrow soup bone**

2 cups chopped **onions**

1 can (28 oz/796 mL) **stewed tomatoes**

8 cups shredded **cabbage**

1¼ tsp **salt**

¼ tsp **pepper**

¼ cup **lemon juice**

3 tbsp **tomato paste**

2 tbsp **granulated sugar**

Cut ribs in half. In Dutch oven, cover ribs and soup bone with water and bring to boil; reduce heat and simmer until meat is no longer pink, about 10 minutes. Drain and rinse ribs and bone; return to pan.

Add onions, tomatoes and 4 cups water; cover and simmer over medium-low heat for 1 hour. Add cabbage, salt and pepper; cover and simmer for 1 hour.

Remove ribs and bone. Remove meat from ribs; trim off fat and chop meat. Remove marrow from bone. Return meat and marrow to pan. Stir in lemon juice, tomato paste and sugar; simmer for 20 minutes.

Makes 10 to 12 servings. PER EACH OF 12 SERVINGS: about 208 cal, 10 g pro, 14 g total fat (5 g sat. fat), 11 g carb, 2 g fibre, 26 mg chol, 355 mg sodium, 365 mg potassium. % RDI: 5% calcium, 11% iron, 2% vit A, 33% vit C, 9% folate.

BEEF & MUSHROOM STEW

Beef stew is never ho-hum when it's got a bit of bacon and plenty of gourmet mushrooms in it. Small, tender button mushrooms are best, but if you can't find them, cut larger white mushrooms into quarters.

Trim and cut beef into 1-inch (2.5 cm) cubes; toss with flour. Sprinkle with salt and pepper. In Dutch oven, heat half of the oil over medium-high heat; brown meat, in batches and adding more oil if necessary. Transfer beef to plate. Add broth to pan and bring to boil, scraping up any browned bits. Transfer liquid to bowl.

In same pan, heat remaining oil over medium heat; fry onion, bacon and thyme for 1 minute. Add button mushrooms; cook until softened and almost no liquid remains, about 8 minutes. Add celery, potatoes, porcini mushrooms, bay leaf, 1 cup water and reserved beef and liquid; bring to boil. Reduce heat, cover and simmer until beef is tender, 1 hour.

Add peas; simmer until hot. Discard bay leaf. *(Make-ahead: Let cool for 30 minutes. Refrigerate, uncovered, in airtight container until cold; cover and refrigerate for up to 2 days.)*

CHANGE IT UP
Slow Cooker Beef & Mushroom Stew

Increase flour to ½ cup. Use ¼ cup of the flour to brown beef; transfer beef to slow cooker. Deglaze skillet with broth as directed; pour liquid into slow cooker. Fry onion, bacon, thyme and button mushrooms as directed; add to slow cooker. Stir in celery, potatoes, porcini mushrooms, bay leaf and 1 cup water. Cover and cook on low until beef is tender, about 6 hours. Whisk remaining flour with ¼ cup water; whisk into slow cooker. Add peas. Cover; cook on high until thickened, about 15 minutes. Discard bay leaf.

2 lb (900 g) **stewing beef cubes**
¼ cup **all-purpose flour**
¾ tsp **salt**
¼ tsp **pepper**
2 tbsp **vegetable oil**
2 cups **sodium-reduced beef broth**
1 **onion,** sliced
2 slices **bacon,** chopped
1 tsp **dried thyme**
4 cups **button mushrooms,** halved (12 oz/340 g)
2 ribs **celery,** chopped
3 cups cubed peeled **potatoes**
1 pkg (14 g) **dried porcini mushrooms**
1 **bay leaf**
1 cup **frozen peas**

Makes 8 servings. PER SERVING: about 370 cal, 27 g pro, 19 g total fat (7 g sat. fat), 23 g carb, 3 g fibre, 71 mg chol, 505 mg sodium, 694 mg potassium. % RDI: 3% calcium, 27% iron, 4% vit A, 13% vit C, 19% folate.

BEEF RAGOUT WITH PENNE RIGATE

Sure, bolognese sauce is great, but this rich beef ragout made with simmering ribs is just divine. When removed from the bone, the meat is meltingly tender. Any short tubular pasta, such as ziti, will catch the sauce inside and out, so feel free to substitute it for the penne if you have it on hand.

Sprinkle short ribs with half each of the salt and pepper. In shallow Dutch oven, heat half of the oil over medium-high heat; brown ribs. Transfer to plate.

Drain fat from pan; add remaining oil and heat over medium heat. Fry onion, carrot, celery, garlic, thyme, bay leaves and remaining salt and pepper, stirring occasionally, until vegetables are softened, about 6 minutes.

Stir in broth, wine and tomatoes; bring to boil. Return ribs to pan; reduce heat, cover and simmer until tender, 2 to 2½ hours. Transfer ribs to plate.

Bring sauce to boil; boil until reduced to about 2½ cups, about 12 minutes.

Meanwhile, remove meat from ribs; dice meat and return to pan. *(Make-ahead: Let cool for 30 minutes. Refrigerate in airtight container until cold; refrigerate, covered, for up to 2 days or freeze for up to 1 month. Reheat to continue.)*

Stir in parsley; simmer until heated through, about 3 minutes. Discard bay leaves.

Meanwhile, in large pot of boiling salted water, cook pasta according to package instructions until al dente. Drain and transfer to serving bowl. Spoon sauce over top.

---

1 lb (450 g) **beef simmering short ribs**
½ tsp each **salt** and **pepper**
2 tbsp **vegetable oil**
1 each **onion, carrot** and rib **celery,** finely diced
2 cloves **garlic,** minced
1 tsp **dried thyme**
2 **bay leaves**
2 cups **sodium-reduced beef broth**
⅔ cup **red wine**
3 **plum tomatoes** (fresh or canned), coarsely chopped
¼ cup chopped **fresh parsley**
4 cups **penne rigate pasta** or ziti pasta

Makes 4 servings. PER SERVING: about 585 cal, 30 g pro, 14 g total fat (4 g sat. fat), 83 g carb, 7 g fibre, 39 mg chol, 922 mg sodium. % RDI: 7% calcium, 45% iron, 39% vit A, 20% vit C, 102% folate.

SWEET & SOUR BRAISED BEEF WITH PRUNES

Spices, prunes and beer combine to make a rich, savoury stew with a touch of enticing sweetness. If you want to substitute beef broth for the beer, reduce the salt by half.

2 tbsp **vegetable oil**

3 lb (1.35 kg) **stewing beef cubes**

2 **onions,** thinly sliced

2 ribs **celery,** thinly sliced

2 cloves **garlic,** minced

2 cups **dark beer** or beef broth

2 cups **beef broth**

½ cup **cider vinegar**

2 tbsp packed **brown sugar**

2 **bay leaves**

1 tsp **salt**

1 tsp **ground ginger**

½ tsp each **ground allspice, cinnamon and nutmeg**

½ tsp **pepper**

¼ tsp **ground cloves**

6 **carrots,** cut in chunks

24 **pitted prunes**

¼ cup **all-purpose flour**

¼ cup **butter,** softened

2 tbsp chopped **fresh parsley**

In Dutch oven, heat half of the oil over medium-high heat; brown beef in 3 batches. Using slotted spoon, transfer to bowl.

Add remaining oil to pan; cook onions, celery and garlic over medium heat, stirring, until onions are softened, about 4 minutes. Return beef and accumulated juices to pan along with beer, broth, vinegar, brown sugar, bay leaves, salt, ginger, allspice, cinnamon, nutmeg, pepper and cloves; bring to boil. Reduce heat; cover and simmer for 1 hour. Stir in carrots and prunes; cook until beef is tender, about 1 hour. Discard bay leaves.

Mash flour with butter until smooth. Add to stew, 1 tbsp at a time, stirring until liquid thickens slightly. Bring to boil; reduce heat and simmer for 5 minutes. *(Make-ahead: Let cool. Cover and refrigerate for up to 3 days or freeze in airtight container for up to 2 weeks; thaw in refrigerator for 24 hours. Reheat over medium heat, stirring occasionally, until hot.)*

Sprinkle with parsley.

Makes 8 servings. PER SERVING: about 513 cal, 41 g pro, 22 g total fat (8 g sat. fat), 39 g carb, 6 g fibre, 99 mg chol, 695 mg sodium. % RDI: 7% calcium, 38% iron, 145% vit A, 10% vit C, 14% folate.

ROASTED ACCORDION NEW POTATOES

Whether they're for entertaining or a relaxed weekend supper with the family, accordion potatoes are so simple to make and so pretty on the plate that you'll want to serve them all the time. Try them with Balsamic-Braised Beef Ribs (page 219) or Garlic Roast Beef & Gravy (page 154).

In saucepan, cover potatoes with cold salted water; bring to boil. Reduce heat to medium-high and simmer until fork-tender, about 10 minutes. Drain and let cool to room temperature. *(Make-ahead: Refrigerate in airtight container for up to 24 hours.)*

Using sharp knife and without cutting all the way through, cut scant ¼-inch (5 mm) thick slices crosswise across each potato, leaving bottom intact. Toss together potatoes, butter, thyme, oil, salt and pepper.

Bake, cut side up, on parchment paper–lined rimmed baking sheet on bottom rack in 350°F (180°C) oven until skins are golden and shrivelled, about 1 hour.

24 **mini yellow-fleshed potatoes** (2 lb/900 g total), scrubbed
2 tbsp **butter,** melted
1 tbsp chopped **fresh thyme**
1 tbsp **olive oil**
½ tsp **salt**
¼ tsp **pepper**

Makes 8 servings. PER SERVING: about 122 cal, 2 g pro, 5 g total fat (2 g sat. fat), 19 g carb, 2 g fibre, 8 mg chol, 388 mg sodium, 362 mg potassium. % RDI: 1% calcium, 6% iron, 3% vit A, 20% vit C, 5% folate.

SLOW COOKER BEEF & BEER

An 8-cup (2 L) slow cooker is just the right size for small batches of stew – and it's perfect for this four-serving recipe. Mashed or boiled potatoes make a tasty side and will soak up all the rich, meaty gravy.

2 lb (900 g) **boneless beef cross rib pot roast**

2 tbsp **vegetable oil**

¼ cup diced **bacon**

2 **carrots,** sliced

2 **onions,** diced

2 cloves **garlic,** minced

3 cups **button mushrooms,** halved (8 oz/225 g total)

¼ tsp each **salt, pepper** and **dried thyme**

¾ cup each **beer** and **sodium-reduced beef broth** (or all beef broth)

2 tbsp **tomato paste**

2 tbsp **all-purpose flour**

¼ cup minced **fresh parsley**

Cut beef into 1½-inch (4 cm) cubes. In large skillet, heat half of the oil over medium-high heat; brown beef. Transfer to slow cooker.

Add bacon to skillet; fry until starting to crisp. Transfer to slow cooker.

Drain fat from skillet; add remaining oil and heat over medium heat. Fry carrots, onions, garlic, mushrooms, salt, pepper and thyme, stirring occasionally, until onions are softened, about 3 minutes. Add beer, stirring and scraping up browned bits; scrape into slow cooker.

Add broth and tomato paste to slow cooker; stir to combine. Cover and cook on low until beef is tender, 6 to 8 hours.

Skim fat from liquid in slow cooker. Whisk flour with ¼ cup water; whisk into slow cooker. Cover and cook on high until thickened, about 15 minutes. Stir in parsley.

Makes 4 servings. PER SERVING: about 444 cal, 52 g pro, 18 g total fat (5 g sat. fat), 18 g carb, 3 g fibre, 110 mg chol, 491 mg sodium. % RDI: 6% calcium, 40% iron, 68% vit A, 17% vit C, 23% folate.

CHANGE IT UP
Oven-Braised Beef & Beer

Omit flour. In shallow Dutch oven, brown beef in oil; set aside. Fry bacon, carrots, onions, garlic, mushrooms, salt, pepper and thyme until vegetables are tender, about 7 minutes. Stir in tomato paste until vegetables are coated. Add beer and broth; bring to boil, stirring and scraping up browned bits. Return meat to pan. Cover and cook in 325°F (160°C) oven, stirring occasionally, until beef is tender, 2½ to 3 hours. Stir in parsley.

SOUTHWESTERN BRAISED BEEF

Good old chili con carne gets a makeover with extra spices and cubed beef, making it special enough for laid-back entertaining. Serve with a chipotle-flavoured hot sauce for heat seekers.

1½ cups **dried red kidney beans**

2 lb (900 g) **beef outside round oven roast**

¼ cup **chili powder**

2 tsp **ground cumin**

1 tsp each **ground coriander** and **dried oregano**

1 tsp **ancho chili powder**

¼ tsp each **ground allspice** and **cinnamon**

3 tbsp **vegetable oil**

2 **onions,** chopped

4 cloves **garlic,** minced

1 can (28 oz/796 mL) **whole tomatoes**

1 tsp **salt**

½ tsp **granulated sugar**

In saucepan, add enough water to cover beans by 1 inch (2.5 cm). Cover and bring to boil; boil for 1 minute. Remove from heat; let stand for 1 hour. (Or soak beans overnight in cold water.) Drain; add enough water to saucepan to cover beans by 3 inches (8 cm); simmer until tender, about 1½ hours. Drain.

Cut roast into ¾-inch (2 cm) cubes. In small bowl, combine chili powder, cumin, coriander, oregano, ancho chili powder, allspice and cinnamon; stir in 2 tbsp of the oil to make paste.

In Dutch oven or large saucepan, heat remaining oil over medium-high heat; brown beef, in batches. Using slotted spoon, transfer to plate.

Drain fat from pan; fry onions and garlic over medium heat, stirring occasionally, until golden, about 5 minutes. Add chili powder mixture; fry until fragrant, about 30 seconds. Add beef; cook, stirring, for 1 minute. Add beans, 2 cups water, tomatoes, salt and sugar, breaking up tomatoes with spoon; bring to boil. Reduce heat, cover and simmer for 1 hour.

Uncover and simmer until slightly thickened and meat is tender, about 30 minutes. *(Make-ahead: Let cool for 30 minutes; freeze in airtight container for up to 2 weeks.)*

Dried kidney beans you cook yourself will hold their shape better in this long-braised dish – canned ones tend to fall apart. If you're in a hurry (or didn't plan ahead), this quick-soak method works really well and saves you from soaking the beans overnight.

Makes 8 to 10 servings. PER EACH OF 10 SERVINGS: about 295 cal, 28 g pro, 10 g total fat (2 g sat. fat), 25 g carb, 7 g fibre, 44 mg chol, 424 mg sodium. % RDI: 7% calcium, 39% iron, 11% vit A, 23% vit C, 51% folate.

SLOW COOKER SPICY TOMATO & BEEF CHILI

**Using stewing beef instead of ground meat turns this classic chili into a chunkier, heartier affair.
Serve it with corn bread or muffins, or use it as a topping for baked potatoes.**

In slow cooker, stir together beef cubes, red kidney beans, tomatoes, beef broth, tomato paste, onion, sugar, chili powder, salt and pepper.

Cover and cook on low until beef is tender, about 7 hours.

Stir in chopped parsley. Ladle into bowls; top with sour cream.

2 lb (900 g) **stewing beef cubes**

2 cans (19 oz/540 mL each) **red kidney beans,** drained and rinsed

1 can (28 oz/796 mL) **whole tomatoes**

1 cup **sodium-reduced beef broth**

¼ cup **tomato paste**

1 **onion,** chopped

1 tbsp **granulated sugar**

2 tsp **chipotle chili powder**

¼ tsp each **salt** and **pepper**

½ cup chopped **fresh parsley**

¾ cup **sour cream**

TIP

Chipotle chili powder is simply ground chipotle peppers (smoke-dried red jalapeño peppers). It gives recipes a spicy, smoky flavour that regular chili powder doesn't add. If you don't have any chipotle chili powder in your spice cupboard, mix together 2 tsp smoked paprika and ¼ tsp cayenne pepper for a similar taste.

Makes 6 to 8 servings. PER EACH OF 8 SERVINGS: about 377 cal, 31 g pro, 16 g total fat (7 g sat. fat), 28 g carb, 9 g fibre, 76 mg chol, 721 mg sodium, 940 mg potassium. % RDI: 10% calcium, 36% iron, 10% vit A, 35% vit C, 32% folate.

SLOW COOKER WINE-BRAISED VEAL SHANKS

Shanks used to be an economical cut favoured by budget watchers, but these days, they have moved up in the world. Anchovies, garlic and lemon add zing to this supereasy dish that's lovely for a classy Sunday dinner.

In shallow dish, stir together flour and half each of the salt and pepper; press veal shanks into flour mixture, turning to coat. Reserve remaining flour mixture.

In large skillet, heat oil over medium-high heat; brown veal, in batches. Transfer to plate.

Drain fat from pan; cook onion, garlic, anchovies, sage and remaining salt and pepper over medium heat, stirring occasionally, until onion is softened, about 5 minutes. Add wine; bring to boil, scraping up browned bits. Scrape into slow cooker.

Add tomatoes, tomato paste, lemon zest and 1 tbsp of the lemon juice to slow cooker; stir to combine. Add veal. Cover and cook on low until veal is tender, 6 to 8 hours.

Using slotted spoon, transfer veal to serving platter; cover and keep warm. Skim fat from liquid in slow cooker. Whisk reserved flour mixture with 3 tbsp water; whisk into liquid. Cover and cook on high until thickened, about 15 minutes.

Discard lemon zest; stir in remaining lemon juice. Pour over veal. Sprinkle with parsley.

¼ cup **all-purpose flour**

½ tsp each **salt** and **pepper**

8 pieces (1 inch/2.5 cm thick) **veal hind shank** (about 4 lb/1.8 kg total)

1 tbsp **extra-virgin olive oil**

1 **onion,** chopped

4 cloves **garlic,** minced

6 **anchovy fillets,** rinsed and minced

1 tbsp crumbled **dried sage**

¾ cup **white wine** or sodium-reduced chicken broth

1 can (28 oz/796 mL) **whole tomatoes,** puréed

¼ cup **tomato paste**

2 strips **lemon zest**

3 tbsp **lemon juice**

¼ cup minced **fresh parsley**

Makes 8 servings. PER SERVING: about 308 cal, 37 g pro, 12 g total fat (4 g sat. fat), 11 g carb, 2 g fibre, 149 mg chol, 542 mg sodium, 945 mg potassium. % RDI: 9% calcium, 26% iron, 4% vit A, 35% vit C, 19% folate.

OSSO BUCO

Down-to-earth but fancy enough for entertaining, this comforting Italian dish braises away to tenderness while you sit back and enjoy your guests' company. Simple polenta (see Tip, opposite) makes a tasty side dish.

6 pieces (1½ inches/4 cm thick) **veal hind shank** (about 3½ lb/1.5 kg total)

2 tbsp **all-purpose flour**

½ tsp each **salt** and **pepper**

2 tbsp **olive oil** (approx)

1 cup each chopped **onion** and **carrot**

⅔ cup chopped **celery**

2 cloves **garlic,** minced

½ tsp each **dried thyme, sage** and **rosemary**

¾ cup **dry white wine**

1½ cups drained **canned whole tomatoes,** coarsely chopped

½ cup **beef broth**

2 **bay leaves**

GREMOLATA:
¼ cup chopped **fresh parsley**

1 tbsp grated **lemon zest**

1 clove **garlic,** minced

Cut six 24-inch (60 cm) lengths of kitchen string; wrap each twice around each shank and tie firmly. On plate, combine flour and half each of the salt and pepper; press veal into flour mixture, turning to coat. Reserve any remaining flour mixture.

In large Dutch oven, heat oil over medium-high heat; brown veal, in batches and adding up to 1 tbsp more oil if necessary. Transfer to plate.

Drain fat from pan; cook onion, carrot, celery, garlic, thyme, sage and rosemary over medium heat, stirring often, until softened, about 10 minutes. Sprinkle with any reserved flour mixture; cook, stirring, for 1 minute. Add wine, stirring and scraping up browned bits. Bring to boil; boil until liquid is reduced by half, 2 minutes.

Stir in tomatoes, broth, bay leaves and remaining salt and pepper. Nestle veal in sauce; bring to boil. Cover and cook in 350°F (180°C) oven, basting every 30 minutes, for 1½ hours. Turn veal and cook, uncovered and basting twice, until tender, about 30 minutes. Using slotted spoon, transfer veal to serving platter; cut off string. Keep warm.

Place pan over medium-high heat; boil sauce gently, stirring, until slightly thickened, about 5 minutes. Discard bay leaves. Pour over veal.

GREMOLATA: Meanwhile, in small bowl, stir together parsley, lemon zest and garlic; sprinkle over veal.

Makes 6 servings. PER SERVING: about 364 cal, 42 g pro, 16 g total fat (5 g sat. fat), 11 g carb, 2 g fibre, 171 mg chol, 576 mg sodium. % RDI: 9% calcium, 25% iron, 36% vit A, 25% vit C, 21% folate.

SLOW COOKER SOUTHERN-STYLE PORK ROAST

This is a fantastic all-purpose braised roast. Serve it as is alongside Roasted Accordion New Potatoes (page 227) or turn it into pulled pork using two forks and pile it high on fluffy buns with barbecue sauce.

In slow cooker, combine onions, garlic, tomatoes, molasses, vinegar, brown sugar, chili powder, salt and pepper. Top with pork.

Cover and cook on low until pork is tender, 6 to 8 hours. Transfer pork to platter; tent with foil. Keep warm.

Whisk flour with ¼ cup water until smooth; whisk into liquid in slow cooker. Cover and cook on high until slightly thickened, about 30 minutes.

Separate pork into portions; serve with sauce.

2 **onions,** thinly sliced

2 cloves **garlic,** minced

1 can (28 oz/796 mL) **diced tomatoes**

⅓ cup **cooking molasses**

¼ cup **cider vinegar**

3 tbsp packed **brown sugar**

2 tsp **chili powder**

1 tsp **salt**

½ tsp **pepper**

3 lb (1.35 kg) **boneless pork shoulder roast**

3 tbsp **all-purpose flour**

Polenta is heavenly with Osso Buco (opposite) or any other stewy, meaty dish. To make 6 servings, in saucepan, bring 6 cups water and ¾ tsp salt to boil. Slowly whisk in 1½ cups cornmeal; cook, stirring often, until thick enough to mound on spoon, 20 to 25 minutes.

Makes 8 servings. PER SERVING: about 316 cal, 22 g pro, 14 g total fat (5 g sat. fat), 26 g carb, 2 g fibre, 76 mg chol, 492 mg sodium, 767 mg potassium. % RDI: 8% calcium, 24% iron, 3% vit A, 25% vit C, 10% folate.

MILK-BRAISED PORK LOIN

Braising in milk may seem unusual, but it's a tradition in Italy. The milk curdles as it cooks but smooths out when it's puréed, creating a creamy, pale golden sauce. If you like, stir in 8 cipollini or 16 pearl onions, peeled, during the last hour of braising. Add them to the platter with the pork before puréeing the sauce.

3 lb (1.35 kg) **centre-cut pork loin rib end roast** or pork shoulder butt roast, tied

½ tsp each **salt** and **pepper**

2 tbsp **vegetable oil**

1 **onion,** chopped

3 cups **milk**

1 tbsp **lemon juice**

2 tbsp chopped **fresh parsley**

Trim fat from pork, leaving ⅛-inch (3 mm) thick layer. Sprinkle pork with salt and pepper. In large Dutch oven, heat oil over medium-high heat; brown pork all over. Transfer to plate.

Drain fat from pan; cook onion over medium heat, stirring often, until golden, about 4 minutes. Add milk, scraping up any browned bits.

Return pork and any accumulated juices to pan; bring to simmer. Cover and braise in 300°F (150°C) oven, basting every 30 minutes and turning once with 2 wooden spoons, until pork is very tender, 2 to 2½ hours.

Transfer to cutting board; tent with foil. Let stand for 10 minutes before cutting strings and slicing across the grain.

Meanwhile, skim fat from sauce. Bring to boil over high heat; boil until reduced to 2½ cups, about 10 minutes. Transfer to blender or food processor; purée until smooth. Blend in lemon juice; stir in parsley. Serve with pork.

Makes 6 to 8 servings. PER EACH OF 8 SERVINGS: about 309 cal, 24 g pro, 21 g total fat (7 g sat. fat), 6 g carb, trace fibre, 74 mg chol, 237 mg sodium. % RDI: 12% calcium, 9% iron, 5% vit A, 3% vit C, 4% folate.

CHANGE IT UP

Slow Cooker Milk-Braised Pork Loin

Brown pork and cook onion and milk as directed. Transfer liquid to slow cooker; top with pork. Cover and cook on low until pork is very tender, about 8 hours. Remove pork for slicing and make sauce as directed.

TANGY COLESLAW

The longer it sits, the more flavourful this slaw gets, so make it a day in advance for the best taste.
This recipe makes plenty for a crowd, so halve it for a smaller (or less hungry) group.

¼ cup **cider vinegar**

1 tbsp **lemon juice**

2 tsp **granulated sugar**

½ tsp **salt**

¼ tsp **pepper**

⅓ cup **extra-virgin olive oil**

10 cups shredded **cabbage**

1½ cups thinly sliced **radishes**

Half **Vidalia onion,** thinly sliced

2 tbsp chopped **fresh parsley**

In large bowl, whisk together vinegar, lemon juice, sugar, salt and pepper until sugar is dissolved. Whisk in oil until combined.

Toss in cabbage, radishes, onion and parsley. Cover and refrigerate for 2 hours. *(Make-ahead: Refrigerate for up to 24 hours.)*

CHANGE IT UP
Tropical Coleslaw

Substitute lime juice for the vinegar and fresh cilantro for the parsley. Add 1 cup diced pineapple and 1 mango, peeled and diced.

Makes 10 to 12 servings. PER EACH OF 12 SERVINGS: about 78 cal, 1 g pro, 6 g total fat (1 g sat. fat), 6 g carb, 1 g fibre, 0 mg chol, 114 mg sodium, 204 mg potassium. % RDI: 3% calcium, 4% iron, 2% vit A, 38% vit C, 15% folate.

PULLED PORK WITH FENNEL BISCUITS

**This biscuit-topped pulled pork – cooked in one dish in the oven – is pure comfort food.
Enjoy it with Tangy Coleslaw (opposite) on the side for a tasty southern barbecue–style dinner.**

Combine half of the brown sugar, the cumin, the oregano, half of the salt, and the pepper; rub all over pork. Let stand for 30 minutes.

In Dutch oven, heat oil over medium-high heat; brown pork. Transfer to plate. Add onion, celery, red pepper, fennel, carrot and garlic to pan; cook over medium heat, stirring often, until softened, 5 to 8 minutes. Add tomatoes, ½ cup water, vinegar, orange zest, and remaining sugar and salt; bring to boil.

Return pork and any accumulated juices to pan; return to boil. Cover and braise in 300°F (150°C) oven, turning once, until pork is tender, 3 hours. Transfer pork to cutting board; tent with foil. Let stand for 10 minutes. With 2 forks, shred or "pull" pork.

Meanwhile, skim fat from sauce; discard orange zest. Simmer over medium heat until reduced to 4 cups, about 15 minutes. Stir shredded pork back into pan. Transfer to 13- x 9-inch (3 L) baking dish.

BISCUITS: In bowl, whisk flour, baking powder, fennel seeds and salt. Using pastry blender, cut in butter until crumbly. Pour buttermilk over top, stirring to form soft ragged dough. Turn out onto lightly floured surface; knead a few times until dough comes together. Shape dough into 12- x 8-inch (30 x 20 cm) rectangle; cut into 12 biscuits.

Arrange biscuits evenly over pork. Whisk egg with 1 tbsp water; brush over biscuits. Bake in 375°F (190°C) oven until biscuits are golden and no longer doughy underneath, 40 to 45 minutes.

¼ cup packed **brown sugar**
2 tsp **ground cumin**
1½ tsp **dried oregano**
1¼ tsp **salt**
1 tsp **pepper**
3 lb (1.35 kg) **pork shoulder blade roast**
2 tbsp **vegetable oil**
1 each **onion**, rib **celery** and **sweet red pepper**, finely diced
1 small bulb **fennel**, finely diced
1 **carrot**, finely diced
3 cloves **garlic**, crushed
1 bottle (680 mL) **strained tomatoes** (passata)
⅓ cup **red wine vinegar**
3 strips **orange zest**

BISCUITS:
2 cups **all-purpose flour**
1 tbsp **baking powder**
1 tsp **fennel seeds**, crushed
¼ tsp **salt**
½ cup cold **butter**, cubed
¾ cup cold **buttermilk** (approx)
1 **egg**

Makes 12 servings. PER SERVING: about 391 cal, 19 g pro, 22 g total fat (9 g sat. fat), 27 g carb, 2 g fibre, 90 mg chol, 618 sodium, 577 mg potassium. % RDI: 10% calcium, 27% iron, 22% vit A, 33% vit C, 20% folate.

PULLED PORK WITH FENNEL BISCUITS page 239

BRAISED PORK SHOULDER & WHITE BEANS

A bone-in pork shoulder picnic roast or boneless pork shoulder butt roast can be used interchangeably in this recipe (if you're using a picnic roast, leave its fat cap on for extra flavour). The acidity of the garlic vinegar cuts through the richness of the pork. Pass it around so each person can add it to taste.

2 cups **dried navy beans** or dried cannellini beans (1 lb/450 g)

4 lb (1.8 kg) **bone-in pork shoulder picnic roast** or boneless pork shoulder butt roast

1 tsp each **salt** and **pepper**

1 tbsp **extra-virgin olive oil**

3 ribs **celery,** diced

2 **carrots,** diced

1 **onion,** diced

5 cloves **garlic,** minced

1 tsp **dried thyme**

½ tsp **dried oregano**

1 **bay leaf**

GARLIC VINEGAR:
2 cloves **garlic,** minced

¼ cup **white wine vinegar**

Pinch **salt**

Rinse beans; soak overnight in 6 cups water. (Or, for quick-soak method, bring to boil and boil gently for 2 minutes. Remove from heat, cover and let stand for 1 hour.) Drain.

In saucepan, cover beans with three times their volume of water and bring to boil. Reduce heat, cover and simmer until tender, about 40 minutes. Reserving 2½ cups of the cooking liquid, drain beans.

Sprinkle pork all over with salt and pepper. In Dutch oven, heat oil over high heat; brown pork all over. Transfer to plate.

Drain all but 1 tbsp fat from pan; cook celery, carrots and onion over medium heat until softened and light golden, about 8 minutes. Stir in garlic, thyme, oregano and bay leaf; cook for 2 minutes. Add beans to pan. Return pork and any juices to pan. Add reserved bean cooking liquid; bring to boil.

Cover and roast in 350°F (180°C) oven for 2½ hours. Uncover; roast until tender, about 30 minutes.

Transfer pork to cutting board; tent with foil. Let stand for 15 minutes before slicing. Discard bay leaf.

GARLIC VINEGAR: Meanwhile, whisk together garlic, vinegar and salt. Serve with pork and beans.

 Beans thicken as they sit, but if they seem too soupy, simmer for a few minutes over medium heat to thicken slightly.

Makes 8 servings. PER SERVING: about 564 cal, 43 g pro, 28 g total fat (9 g sat. fat), 35 g carb, 10 g fibre, 121 mg chol, 449 mg sodium, 1,333 mg potassium. % RDI: 12% calcium, 49% iron, 33% vit A, 7% vit C, 50% folate.

CHILI PULLED PORK

Unsweetened chocolate adds richness and depth to this dish inspired by the varied mole sauces of Mexico. Serve on buns or, better yet, in warm corn tortillas for the most authentic experience.

In Dutch oven, heat oil over medium-high heat. Sprinkle pork with 1 tsp of the salt; brown pork all over. Transfer to plate.

Drain all but 1 tbsp fat from pan; cook onions and garlic, stirring occasionally, until softened, about 5 minutes. Add tomatoes, 1 cup water, vinegar, chili powder, molasses, brown sugar, oregano, cumin, coriander, pepper and remaining salt; bring to boil, scraping up browned bits. Stir in chocolate until melted.

Return pork and any accumulated juices to pan; bring to boil. Cover and braise in 300°F (150°C) oven, turning once, until tender, about 3 hours.

Transfer pork to large bowl; tent with foil. Let stand for 15 minutes. With 2 forks, shred or "pull" pork, discarding skin and fat.

Skim fat from sauce. Return pork to sauce and heat until bubbling.

CHANGE IT UP
Chili Braised Brisket

Replace pork with 4 lb (1.8 kg) beef brisket. Omit browning. Place brisket in roasting pan; pour sauce over top, turning to coat. Cover and braise in 325°F (160°C) oven until fork-tender, about 3½ hours. Transfer to cutting board; tent with foil. Let stand for 10 minutes before slicing across the grain. Serve with sauce.

2 tbsp **vegetable oil**

3 lb (1.35 kg) **boneless pork shoulder roast**

1½ tsp **salt**

3 **onions,** chopped

4 cloves **garlic,** minced

1½ cups bottled **strained tomatoes** (passata)

⅓ cup **cider vinegar**

¼ cup **chili powder**

¼ cup **fancy molasses**

2 tbsp packed **dark brown sugar**

1 tsp **dried oregano**

1 tsp each **ground cumin** and **ground coriander**

¼ tsp **pepper**

1 oz (30 g) **unsweetened chocolate,** chopped

Makes 8 to 10 servings. PER EACH OF 10 SERVINGS: about 377 cal, 25 g pro, 23 g total fat (19 g sat. fat), 18 g carb, 2 g fibre, 92 mg chol, 611 mg sodium, 713 mg potassium. % RDI: 8% calcium, 29% iron, 11% vit A, 7% vit C, 7% folate.

SLOW COOKER BLACK BEAN SPARERIBS

You'll find bite-size bone-in pork spareribs at most Asian grocery stores, or you can order them at the butcher counter. Serve them with steamed rice and sautéed baby bok choy.

In slow cooker, stir together spareribs, 1¼ cups water, onion, black bean garlic sauce, garlic, ginger, chili garlic paste and pepper. Cover and cook on low until ribs are tender, about 6 hours. With slotted spoon, transfer ribs to plate.

Skim fat from liquid in slow cooker. Stir cornstarch with 2 tbsp water; stir into liquid. Cover and cook on high until thickened, about 20 minutes.

Return ribs to slow cooker, stirring to coat. Sprinkle with green onion.

3 lb (1.35 kg) **bite-size bone-in pork spareribs**

1 **onion,** finely diced

2 tbsp **black bean garlic sauce**

4 cloves **garlic,** minced

1 tbsp minced **fresh ginger**

½ tsp **chili garlic paste** (such as sambal oelek)

½ tsp **pepper**

2 tbsp **cornstarch**

1 **green onion,** thinly sliced

Black bean garlic sauce gets its distinctive earthiness from fermented black soybeans, which are salted and left to ferment, giving them a pungent smell and a complex flavour. The beans are then combined with soy sauce, garlic and other seasonings to make this Asian seasoning paste. It keeps almost indefinitely in the fridge and is a terrific pantry ingredient to have on hand for stir-fries and Chinese dishes like these ribs.

Makes 6 to 8 servings. PER EACH OF 8 SERVINGS: about 254 cal, 24 g pro, 15 g total fat (5 g sat. fat), 5 g carb, trace fibre, 78 mg chol, 415 mg sodium, 361 mg potassium. % RDI: 4% calcium, 13% iron, 1% vit A, 2% vit C, 3% folate.

PORK & GRAINY MUSTARD STEW

Garlic and thyme, mustard and wine – these are the perfect seasonings for a comforting autumn pork stew. The stew develops an even fuller flavour when it's cooked ahead of time, making it great for reheating on a busy evening.

3 lb (1.35 kg) **pork braising cubes** or boneless pork shoulder blade roast, cubed

2 tbsp **all-purpose flour**

3 tbsp **vegetable oil**

2 **onions,** chopped

4 **carrots,** chopped

2 ribs **celery,** chopped

2 cloves **garlic,** minced

1 tsp **dried thyme**

¼ tsp each **salt** and **pepper**

2 cups **sodium-reduced chicken broth**

½ cup **white wine** or sodium-reduced chicken broth

1 **bay leaf**

¼ cup **grainy mustard**

¾ cup **frozen peas**

¼ cup minced **fresh parsley**

Toss pork with 1 tbsp of the flour. In Dutch oven, heat half of the oil over medium-high heat; brown pork, in batches, adding more oil as needed. Transfer to plate.

Add remaining oil to pan; cook onions, carrots, celery, garlic, thyme, salt and pepper, stirring often, until softened, about 5 minutes.

Add broth, wine, bay leaf and 1½ cups water; return pork and any accumulated juices to pan. Bring to boil; reduce heat, cover and simmer, stirring occasionally, until pork is tender, about 45 minutes. Discard bay leaf.

Whisk together mustard, remaining flour and 2 tbsp water; stir into stew and simmer until thickened, about 3 minutes. Stir in peas and parsley; cook until heated through, about 3 minutes. *(Make-ahead: Let cool for 30 minutes; refrigerate in airtight container for up to 3 days or freeze for up to 1 month.)*

Makes 8 servings. PER SERVING: about 315 cal, 37 g pro, 13 g total fat (3 g sat. fat), 11 g carb, 2 g fibre, 109 mg chol, 480 mg sodium. % RDI: 5% calcium, 23% iron, 69% vit A, 12% vit C, 15% folate.

SOUTHWEST PULLED PORK CHILI SOUP

This hearty soup version of pulled pork has a smoky tomato broth with a little chili kick. Corn bread (plain or with minced jalapeños) or Buttermilk Scones (page 250) are tasty partners.

PULLED PORK STOCK: Sprinkle pork with salt and pepper. In Dutch oven or large saucepan, heat oil over medium-high heat; brown pork all over. Add 6 cups water, tomatoes, onion, peppercorns and bay leaf; bring to boil. Reduce heat, cover and simmer until pork is tender, 2½ to 3 hours. Transfer pork to cutting board; tent with foil. Let stand for 20 minutes.

With 2 forks, shred or "pull" pork and place in large bowl; discard skin and fat. Strain stock into large measure to make about 6 cups; skim off fat. Add stock to pork. *(Make-ahead: Refrigerate in airtight container for up to 24 hours.)*

Meanwhile, broil green peppers and jalapeño peppers, turning often, until charred and blackened, 10 to 20 minutes. Let cool; peel, seed and finely chop.

In Dutch oven, heat oil over medium heat; cook onions, stirring occasionally, until softened, 4 to 6 minutes. Add garlic; cook until golden, 1 to 2 minutes. Stir in tomato paste, chili powder, salt, cumin and pepper. Add chopped peppers and pulled pork stock; bring to boil. Reduce heat, cover and simmer to meld flavours, about 10 minutes.

4 **sweet green peppers**

4 **jalapeño peppers**

2 tbsp **olive oil** or vegetable oil

2 **onions,** chopped

3 cloves **garlic,** minced

1 tbsp **tomato paste**

1½ tsp **ancho chili powder** or chili powder

1 tsp each **salt** and **ground cumin**

¼ tsp **pepper**

PULLED PORK STOCK:

2½ lb (1.125 kg) **boneless pork shoulder roast**

¼ tsp each **salt** and **pepper**

1 tbsp **olive oil**

1½ cups **bottled strained tomatoes** (passata)

1 **onion,** halved

5 **black peppercorns**

1 **bay leaf**

Makes 10 to 12 servings. PER EACH OF 12 SERVINGS: about 178 cal, 13 g pro, 11 g total fat (3 g sat. fat), 7 g carb, 1 g fibre, 46 mg chol, 316 mg sodium, 299 mg potassium. % RDI: 3% calcium, 12% iron, 3% vit A, 53% vit C, 6% folate.

SLOW COOKER PORK & BLACK BEAN CHILI

This chili is a weeknight champion. The salsa gives it a nice hit of fresh flavour and is so simple you'll want to make it all the time for topping tacos or burritos (or eating straight up with tortilla chips).

4 slices **thick-cut bacon,** cut crosswise into strips

1¼ lb (565 g) **boneless pork loin centre roast,** cubed

1 tbsp **vegetable oil**

2 **onions,** diced

1 each **carrot** and **sweet green pepper,** diced

4 cloves **garlic,** minced

1½ tsp each **dried oregano** and **ground cumin**

¼ tsp each **salt** and **pepper**

2 cans (each 19 oz/540 mL) **black beans,** drained and rinsed

½ cup **bottled strained tomatoes** (passata)

SALSA:

½ cup chopped **cherry tomatoes** or grape tomatoes

Half **sweet yellow pepper** or sweet orange pepper, diced

1 **green onion,** thinly sliced

1 tbsp **lime juice**

In large skillet, cook bacon over medium heat until golden, about 8 minutes. Using slotted spoon, transfer to paper towel–lined plate. Drain all but 1 tbsp fat from pan; brown pork, in batches. Transfer bacon and pork to slow cooker.

Add oil to pan; cook onions, carrot, green pepper, garlic, oregano, cumin, salt and pepper over medium heat until golden, about 10 minutes. Add to slow cooker.

Add beans, tomatoes and 2 cups water to slow cooker; cover and cook on low until pork is tender, 6 to 8 hours.

SALSA: In bowl, combine tomatoes, yellow pepper, green onion and lime juice; serve with chili.

Makes 6 servings. PER SERVING: about 363 cal, 33 g pro, 11 g total fat (3 g sat. fat), 34 g carb, 12 g fibre, 65 mg chol, 781 mg sodium. % RDI: 9% calcium, 31% iron, 25% vit A, 70% vit C, 45% folate.

BUTTERMILK SCONES

This scone is a recipe box essential. It's the ideal fluffy companion to soups, stews and braised dishes of all kinds. These scones are also a terrific all-purpose foundation for fruit shortcakes during berry or peach season.

2½ cups **all-purpose flour**

2 tbsp **granulated sugar**

2½ tsp **baking powder**

½ tsp **baking soda**

½ tsp **salt**

½ cup cold **butter,** cubed

1 cup **buttermilk**

1 **egg**

In bowl, whisk together flour, sugar, baking powder, baking soda and salt. Using pastry blender or 2 knives, cut in butter until in coarse crumbs with a few larger pieces. Whisk buttermilk with egg; using fork, stir into flour mixture just until dough forms.

Turn out onto lightly floured surface; knead gently 10 times. Pat out into 10- x 7-inch (25 x 18 cm) rectangle; trim edges to straighten. Cut into 6 squares; cut each diagonally in half.

Place, 1 inch (2.5 cm) apart, on parchment paper–lined baking sheet. Bake in 400°F (200°C) oven until golden, 12 to 15 minutes.

Buttermilk is something you don't always have on hand. But not to worry! You can still make these scones using this simple substitution: Pour 1 tbsp vinegar or lemon juice into glass measuring cup; pour in enough milk to make 1 cup. Stir to combine, then let the mixture stand for 5 minutes to thicken up a bit. Use in place of 1 cup buttermilk in any baking recipe.

Makes 12 scones. PER SCONE: about 189 cal, 4 g pro, 9 g total fat (5 g sat. fat), 23 g carb, 1 g fibre, 37 mg chol, 289 mg sodium. % RDI: 6% calcium, 9% iron, 8% vit A, 26% folate.

HAM HOCK SQUASH SOUP

Ham hock is a tantalizing base for soup – here, the bone makes a flavourful stock for cooking the chickpeas, and the meat adds a nice texture to the finished soup. Look for meaty ham hocks at the butcher counter. If your hock is bigger than 2 lb (900 g), cut it into portions and freeze the rest for more soup down the road.

In large saucepan, bring chickpeas and 4 cups water to boil; boil for 3 minutes. Remove from heat; cover and let stand for 1 hour. (Or soak chickpeas in 4 cups water overnight.) Drain and rinse under cold water.

Poke cloves into 1 onion half. In Dutch oven, bring onion halves, 8 cups water, chickpeas, ham hock, garlic and bay leaf to boil; reduce heat, cover and simmer, skimming off foam, for 1½ hours.

Add carrot, chopped onion, celery and salt; simmer for 15 minutes. Add squash; simmer until ham hock is tender, about 30 minutes. Discard onion halves and bay leaf.

Remove ham hock; discard fat and bone. Cut meat (and skin, if desired) into bite-size pieces and return to pan. Add pepper and heat through, adding more water if too thick.

CHANGE IT UP
Smoked Turkey Squash Soup

Substitute smoked turkey thigh or drumstick for ham hock.

¾ cup **dried chickpeas**
3 **whole cloves**
1 **onion,** halved
2 lb (900 g) **smoked ham hock**
3 cloves **garlic**
1 **bay leaf**
1 cup chopped **carrot**
1 cup chopped **onion**
½ cup chopped **celery**
1 tsp **salt**
1 **butternut squash** (about 1 lb/450 g), peeled and chopped
¼ tsp **pepper**

Makes 10 to 12 servings. PER EACH OF 12 SERVINGS: about 112 cal, 11 g pro, 3 g total fat (1 g sat. fat), 13 g carb, 2 g fibre, 21 mg chol, 443 mg sodium, 330 mg potassium. % RDI: 4% calcium, 11% iron, 51% vit A, 10% vit C, 25% folate.

Choucroute Garnie With Pork Roast

Replace smoked pork shoulder with regular pork roast. Untie string. Season pork with 1½ tsp salt and ½ tsp pepper; rub inside with 2 cloves garlic, minced, and 2 tsp chopped fresh thyme. Roll and re-tie pork with string; cover and refrigerate for 4 hours. *(Make-ahead: Cover and refrigerate for up to 24 hours.)*

In large cast-iron or heavy skillet, heat 2 tsp vegetable oil over medium-high heat; brown pork roast. Follow recipe, nestling pork into onions.

CHOUCROUTE GARNIE

This French casserole features pork in nearly every form. There are as many variations on this recipe as there are stars in the sky – the key is to find a butcher with beautiful charcuterie (such as bacon, sausages, smoked meats and wieners) and make the dish your own.

In large Dutch oven, melt butter over medium heat; cook onions, stirring, until golden, about 10 minutes. Cut bacon into 6 equal chunks; add to pan and cook until browned and fat is rendered, about 6 minutes.

Add carrot, wine, ½ cup water, bay leaf and caraway seeds. In cheesecloth square, tie together juniper berries, peppercorns and cloves; add to pan. Stir in garlic. Add pork shoulder and sausages; cover with sauerkraut. Cover and cook until warmed through.

Transfer to 325°F (160°C) oven. Cook, turning pork halfway through and re-covering with sauerkraut, until pork is tender, 2½ to 3 hours. Add wieners; cook until heated through, about 15 minutes. Discard bay leaf and spice bag. Transfer bacon, pork, sausages and wieners to cutting board; cut into portions.

Meanwhile, in pot of boiling salted water, cook potatoes until tender, about 15 minutes. Drain.

Heap sauerkraut on large platter; surround with vegetables and meat.

¼ cup **butter**

3 large **onions,** sliced

12 oz (340 g) slab **smoked bacon**

1 large **carrot,** peeled and halved

2 cups **dry Riesling wine**

1 **bay leaf**

1 tsp **caraway seeds**

8 **juniper berries**

6 **black peppercorns**

2 **whole cloves**

2 cloves **garlic**

2 lb (900 g) **smoked pork shoulder roast** or 3 lb (1.35 kg) smoked ham hocks

3 **smoked pork sausages** (such as Strasbourg, bratwurst, frankfurter, knackwurst or blutwurst)

6 cups **sauerkraut,** rinsed, drained and squeezed dry

3 **wieners**

3 large **potatoes,** peeled and halved

Makes 10 to 12 servings. PER EACH OF 12 SERVINGS: about 523 cal, 23 g pro, 37 g total fat (17 g sat. fat), 28 g carb, 5 g fibre, 105 mg chol, 1,608 mg sodium. % RDI: 7% calcium, 25% iron, 17% vit A, 36% vit C, 19% folate.

LAMB SHANKS BRAISED IN BALSAMIC TOMATO SAUCE

In summer, try cooking these meaty shanks with fresh ripe tomatoes, basil and garlic from your own garden. No green thumb? Check out farmer's markets for the best locally grown produce. Herbes de Provence blends sometimes contain lavender, so read the label if that's not your favourite herb.

4 **lamb shanks** (about 1½ lb/675 g total)
1 tsp **herbes de Provence**
½ tsp **salt**
¼ tsp **pepper**
1 tbsp **extra-virgin olive oil**

BALSAMIC TOMATO SAUCE:
1 tbsp **extra-virgin olive oil**
1 **onion,** diced
3 cloves **garlic,** minced
1 **bay leaf**
¼ tsp each **salt** and **pepper**
¼ tsp **dried oregano**
1 can (28 oz/796 mL) **whole tomatoes**
2 tbsp each **granulated sugar** and **balsamic vinegar**
2 tbsp **tomato paste**
1 sprig **fresh basil** (or ½ tsp dried)

Rub lamb all over with herbes de Provence, salt and pepper. Cover and refrigerate for 4 hours. *(Make-ahead: Refrigerate for up to 24 hours.)*

In large skillet, heat oil over medium-high heat; brown lamb, in batches. Transfer to plate.

BALSAMIC TOMATO SAUCE: In Dutch oven, heat oil over medium-high heat; sauté onion until softened, about 5 minutes. Add garlic, bay leaf, salt, pepper and oregano; sauté for 2 minutes. Add tomatoes, breaking up with spoon. Stir in sugar, vinegar, tomato paste and basil; bring to simmer. Add lamb and any accumulated juices; return to simmer.

Cover and braise in 325°F (160°C) oven, basting occasionally, until lamb is tender, about 1½ hours. Transfer lamb to plate; keep warm.

Skim fat from sauce. Bring sauce to boil; reduce heat and simmer until thickened and reduced to about 3 cups, about 10 minutes. Discard bay leaf and basil. Serve sauce with lamb.

Makes 4 servings. PER SERVING: about 264 cal, 20 g pro, 11 g total fat (3 g sat. fat), 23 g carb, 3 g fibre, 53 mg chol, 772 mg sodium, 821 mg potassium. % RDI: 9% calcium, 27% iron, 4% vit A, 53% vit C, 25% folate.

LAMB STOCK

This stock is a key ingredient in Lamb Korma (page 256), but there's plenty left for soups, stews, pilafs and risottos. It freezes well, so it's worth making a big batch when you have the time.

In Dutch oven, bring mutton and 10 cups water to boil. Skim off foam. Add onion, turnip, carrot, celery, garlic, parsley, thyme, bay leaf, salt and peppercorns. Reduce heat and simmer, skimming surface occasionally, until mutton is very tender, about 1½ hours.

Strain into large bowl; skim fat from surface. *(Make-ahead: Let cool for 30 minutes. Refrigerate in airtight containers for up to 3 days or freeze for up to 1 month.)*

Remove meat from bones and save for another use.

3 lb (1.35 kg) **bone-in mutton necks,** lamb necks or stewing lamb cubes

1 **onion,** quartered

1 **white turnip,** peeled and sliced

1 each **carrot** and rib **celery,** chopped

1 clove **garlic,** smashed

3 each sprigs **fresh parsley** and **fresh thyme**

1 **bay leaf**

½ tsp each **salt** and **black peppercorns**

Mutton has a stronger flavour than lamb, and it makes a rich, fragrant stock. Mutton bones aren't always easy to find, however, so you may have to order them from your butcher. Stock made from mutton may be a little gamier than you normally like, so substitute lamb necks or stewing lamb if you prefer a more delicate, less earthy stock.

Makes 8 cups. PER 1 CUP: about 29 cal, 4 g pro, 1 g total fat (trace sat. fat), 2 g carb, trace fibre, 4 mg chol, 144 mg sodium. % RDI: 1% calcium, 2% iron, 1% vit A, 22% vit C.

LAMB KORMA

This rich, classic northern Indian curry is amazingly flavourful and a good challenge for experienced cooks who want to try something new. A heavy-bottomed pot is essential here. If you use a thin-bottomed pot, it can develop hot spots, which can cause the dairy-based sauce to stick if it's not stirred constantly.

⅔ cup **unsalted raw cashews**

⅓ cup **vegetable oil**

6 **onions,** thinly sliced

4 lb (1.8 kg) **boneless lamb shoulder roast**

¾ tsp **salt**

¼ tsp **pepper**

4 **green finger hot peppers** or jalapeño peppers, seeded and minced

2 **bay leaves**

2 tbsp each finely minced **garlic** and **fresh ginger**

1 tbsp **ground coriander**

1 tbsp **garam masala**

⅓ cup **Balkan-style plain yogurt**

½ tsp **ground mace** (or ¼ tsp nutmeg)

½ tsp **cayenne pepper**

3 cups **Lamb Stock** (page 255) or water

1 tbsp **rose water** or water

¼ tsp **saffron threads**

1 tbsp **lime juice**

In dry large skillet, toast cashews over medium heat until well browned. Transfer to food processor; pulse until fine. Set aside in food processor.

In same skillet, heat ¼ cup of the oil over medium heat; cook onions, stirring occasionally, until deep golden, about 20 minutes. Let cool. Add to cashews; purée until smooth.

Meanwhile, cut lamb into 1-inch (2.5 cm) cubes; toss with half each of the salt and pepper. In same skillet, brown lamb, in batches, over medium-high heat; transfer to bowl. Add ⅓ cup water to pan, scraping up any browned bits. Pour over lamb.

In Dutch oven, heat remaining oil over medium heat; fry hot peppers, bay leaves, garlic and ginger for 5 minutes, stirring often and adding up to 2 tbsp water if mixture sticks to pan. Add coriander; fry, stirring, for 2 minutes.

Add garam masala; fry, stirring, for 30 seconds. Stir in yogurt, mace and cayenne pepper; cook, stirring, for 5 minutes. Whisk in stock, onion mixture and remaining salt and pepper.

Add lamb and any accumulated juices to pan; bring to boil. Reduce heat, cover and simmer, stirring often, until lamb is tender and sauce is darkened and thickened, about 1½ hours. Discard bay leaves.

Meanwhile, warm rose water in microwave at high for 30 seconds. Stir in saffron; let stand for 15 minutes. Stir into lamb mixture along with lime juice. *(Make-ahead: Let cool for 30 minutes; refrigerate in airtight container for up to 3 days.)*

Makes 8 servings. PER SERVING: about 539 cal, 50 g pro, 31 g total fat (8 g sat. fat), 16 g carb, 2 g fibre, 153 mg chol, 440 mg sodium. % RDI: 8% calcium, 38% iron, 2% vit A, 15% vit C, 24% folate.

WHOLE SPELT SODA BREAD

Soda bread is an Irish tradition, and it's scrumptious with Slow Cooker Irish Lamb Stew (opposite). Spelt is an ancient variety of wheat that is high in dietary fibre, so this loaf is virtuous as well as tasty.

2½ cups **whole spelt flour**
2 tbsp **granulated sugar**
1¼ tsp **baking soda**
½ tsp **salt**
2 tbsp cold **butter,** cubed
1 **egg white**
⅔ cup **buttermilk**

In large bowl, whisk together flour, sugar, baking soda and salt. Using pastry blender or 2 knives, cut in butter until in coarse crumbs.

Whisk egg white with buttermilk; with fork, stir into flour mixture to form soft dough.

On lightly floured surface and with floured hands, press dough into ball; knead gently 10 times. Place on greased baking sheet; gently pat out into 6-inch (15 cm) circle. Dust top with flour; score with large X.

Bake in 375°F (190°C) oven until lightly browned and cake tester inserted in centre comes out clean, 35 to 40 minutes. Transfer to rack; let cool.

Makes 6 to 8 servings. PER EACH OF 8 SERVINGS: about 175 cal, 6 g pro, 4 g total fat (2 g sat. fat), 31 g carb, 5 g fibre, 10 mg chol, 385 mg sodium. % RDI: 3% calcium, 11% iron, 3% vit A, 5% folate.

SLOW COOKER IRISH LAMB STEW

Traditional Irish stew is a hearty dish that warms you up on a cold night. Adding stout gives it a rich, dark colour and flavour. If you don't have stout on hand, substitute the same amount of your favourite beer.

In slow cooker, combine lamb, potatoes, onions, garlic, broth, stout, tomato paste, rosemary, salt and pepper. Cover and cook on low until lamb is tender, 6 to 8 hours.

Whisk flour with 3 tbsp water until smooth; whisk into slow cooker. Cover and cook on high until thickened, about 15 minutes. Serve sprinkled with parsley.

2 lb (900 g) **stewing lamb cubes,** trimmed

4 large **yellow-fleshed potatoes,** peeled and cubed

2 large **onions,** diced

6 cloves **garlic,** minced

1 cup **sodium-reduced beef broth**

1 cup **Irish stout**

¼ cup **tomato paste**

1½ tsp **dried rosemary**

½ tsp **salt**

¼ tsp **pepper**

3 tbsp **all-purpose flour**

½ cup chopped **fresh parsley**

To add extra rich flavour to this stew, brown the lamb in a little bit of oil before adding it to the slow cooker.

Makes 8 to 10 servings. PER EACH OF 10 SERVINGS: about 358 cal, 22 g pro, 7 g total fat (3 g sat. fat), 31 g carb, 3 g fibre, 65 mg chol, 251 mg sodium, 821 mg potassium. % RDI: 4% calcium, 15% iron, 4% vit A, 25% vit C, 21% folate.

LIMA BEAN & LAMB STEW

There are a lot of spices in this stew, but they're a pared-down version of the traditional North African spice blend *ras el hanout*, which can combine up to 50 different spices. Serve over couscous or rice.

Rinse lima beans; soak overnight in 4½ cups water. (Or, for quick-soak method, bring to boil and boil gently for 2 minutes. Remove from heat, cover and let stand for 1 hour.) Reserving 1 cup of the cooking liquid, drain lima beans.

Trim fat off lamb; cut meat into 1-inch (2.5 cm) cubes. In Dutch oven, heat half of the oil over high heat; brown lamb, in batches. Transfer to plate.

Drain any fat from pan; heat remaining oil over medium heat. Cook onions and garlic, stirring occasionally, until softened, about 6 minutes. Stir in salt, cumin, coriander, ginger, turmeric, cinnamon, cardamom, pepper, saffron, cayenne pepper and cloves; cook, stirring, for 2 minutes.

Stir in reserved cooking liquid, scraping up browned bits. Return lamb and any accumulated juices to pan. Add tomatoes, breaking up with spoon; stir in lima beans, tomato paste and lemon zest. Bring to boil. Reduce heat, cover and simmer until lamb is tender, about 1 hour.

Stir in olives; simmer, uncovered, for 10 minutes. Stir in parsley; cook for 1 minute.

1½ cups **dried large lima beans**

3 lb (1.35 kg) **boneless leg of lamb**

¼ cup **vegetable oil**

2 **onions,** chopped

3 cloves **garlic,** smashed

½ tsp each **salt, ground cumin, ground coriander** and **ground ginger**

¼ tsp each **turmeric, cinnamon** and **ground cardamom**

¼ tsp **pepper**

Pinch each **saffron, cayenne pepper** and **ground cloves**

1 can (28 oz/796 mL) **whole tomatoes**

¼ cup **tomato paste**

2 strips **lemon zest**

½ cup quartered **green olives**

⅓ cup chopped **fresh parsley**

Makes 6 to 8 servings. PER EACH OF 8 SERVINGS: about 376 cal, 36 g pro, 15 g total fat (3 g sat. fat), 25 g carb, 5 g fibre, 93 mg chol, 513 mg sodium. % RDI: 8% calcium, 42% iron, 7% vit A, 45% vit C, 24% folate.

ACKNOWLEDGMENTS

This book is a collaboration between dozens of people. Without their hard work and dedication, it just wouldn't be the same sizzling success it is.

First, a huge thank-you goes to The Canadian Living Test Kitchen. Our fearless Food director, Annabelle Waugh, is always the first person to get me revved up for a cookbook project, and she plunged into this one with her customary gusto and sense of humour. Working with her in the kitchen were our team of Food specialists – Rheanna Kish, Amanda Barnier, Irene Fong, Jennifer Bartoli – and our consulting Food specialist, Melanie Stuparyk. All are true carnivores and the brains (and tastebuds) behind the scrumptious recipes between these covers. Without this team, there would be no Tested-Till-Perfect recipes.

Our two brilliant art directors, Chris Bond and Colin Elliott, get a huge helping of gratitude for their gorgeous design. Colin especially took the ball and ran with it, producing page after page of amazing graphics and tying everything up in a beautiful ribbon (or butcher's twine, in this case).

Photography is what makes these books so sumptuous, and I'm grateful to photographer Edward Pond, food stylists Claire Stubbs and Nicole Young, and prop stylists Catherine Doherty and Madeleine Johari for creating an array of gorgeous images specially for this volume. Their work and the efforts of many other photographers and stylists (see page 270 for more) is what makes the recipes jump off the pages – and into your imagination.

Thanks on this book also go to Janet Rowe for her editorial help – jumping in midstream is never easy, but Janet was her usual patient and thorough self. Copy editor Brenda Thompson went through every page when we were done and made sure each recipe was in perfect shape. Any errors are mine, not hers.

Next, thanks go to Beth Zabloski, who dug into the task of creating a helpful index with customary good cheer, and to Sharyn Joliat of Info Access, who analyzed the nutrient content of each recipe so you can be sure of what you're getting in each bite. Thank you also to the team at Random House Canada, who took the finished book and made sure it got into bookstores and kitchens across the country.

Without the support and encouragement of our management team, this and all of our other cookbooks would never have come to be. I would like to thank Transcontinental Books vice-president Marc Laberge, publishing director Mathieu de Lajartre and assistant editor Céline Comtois for their dedication and hard work on everything from idea to finished product.

Finally, a huge helping of thanks go to *Canadian Living* group publisher Caroline Andrews, associate publisher Susan Antonacci and editor-in-chief Jennifer Reynolds for their confidence in our work, and for giving us the chance to create and innovate with each new book.

– *Tina Anson Mine, project editor*

Our Tested-Till-Perfect guarantee means we've tested every recipe, using the same grocery store ingredients and household appliances as you do, until we're sure you'll get perfect results at home.

About Our Nutrition Information

To meet nutrient needs each day, moderately active women 25 to 49 need about 1,900 calories, 51 g protein, 261 g carbohydrate, 25 to 35 g fibre and not more than 63 g total fat (21 g saturated fat). Men and teenagers usually need more. Canadian sodium intake of approximately 3,500 mg daily should be reduced, whereas the intake of potassium from food sources should be increased to 4,700 mg per day.

Percentage of recommended daily intake (% RDI) is based on the values used for Canadian food labels for calcium, iron, vitamins A and C, and folate.

Figures are rounded off. They are based on the first ingredient listed when there is a choice and do not include optional ingredients or those with no specified amounts.

ABBREVIATIONS:
cal = calories
pro = protein
carb = carbohydrate
sat. fat = saturated fat
chol = cholesterol

CREDITS

RECIPES

ALL RECIPES DEVELOPED BY
THE CANADIAN LIVING TEST KITCHEN.

ILLUSTRATIONS

Colin Elliott: pages 6, 9, 10, 12 and 14.

PHOTOGRAPHY

Michael Alberstat: page 237.

Ryan Brook: back cover (portrait); pages 5, 54, 64, 96, 101 and 119.

Jeff Coulson: pages 51, 80, 93, 104, 138, 187, 201, 218 and 244.

Yvonne Duivenvoorden: pages 19, 27, 30, 43, 72, 77, 145, 158, 169, 176, 182, 224, 229 and 252.

Getty Images: pages 7, 8, 16, 142 and 204.

Joe Kim: pages 61, 69, 85, 88, 122, 164, 165, 188 and 209.

Edward Pond: front cover; back cover (food); pages 58, 59, 108, 109, 111, 127, 130, 137, 147, 153, 161, 173, 181, 212, 216, 232, 240, 241 and 257.

Jodi Pudge: pages 46, 135, 150, 197 and 249.

David Scott: pages 22 and 260.

Stock Food/Jim Norton: page 221.

Ryan Szulc: pages 38 and 114.

Thinkstock: pages 2 and 4.

Veer: pages 6 and 74.

Felix Wedgwood: page 35.

FOOD STYLING

Ashley Denton: pages 69, 85, 88, 122, 127 and 153.

David Grenier: pages 38, 64, 101 and 114.

Adele Hagan: pages 46 and 221.

Lucie Richard: pages 22, 27, 30, 77, 111, 135, 158, 176, 182, 197 and 260.

Claire Stancer: pages 72, 188, 209, 237 and 252.

Claire Stubbs: front cover; back cover (left and right); pages 19, 35, 43, 80, 93, 104, 137, 138, 145, 147, 161, 164, 165, 169, 173, 181, 187, 201, 216, 218, 224, 229 and 244.

Melanie Stuparyk: pages 51, 54, 96 and 119.

Nicole Young: back cover (centre); pages 58, 59, 61, 108, 109, 130, 150, 212, 232, 240, 241, 249 and 257.

PROP STYLING

Martine Blackhurst: page 35.

Laura Branson: pages 22, 46, 51, 61, 64, 69, 85, 88, 96, 104, 119, 188, 209 and 221.

Catherine Doherty: front cover; back cover (food, left and right); pages 72, 111, 122, 127, 137, 147, 153, 161, 181, 182, 197, 201, 216, 218, 244 and 252.

Marc-Philippe Gagné: page 176.

Madeleine Johari: back cover (food, centre); pages 38, 43, 58, 59, 80, 93, 108, 109, 114, 130, 138, 164, 165, 187, 212, 232, 240, 241 and 257.

Karen Kirk: pages 54 and 101.

Chareen Parsons: page 237.

Oksana Slavutych: pages 27, 30, 145, 150, 158, 169, 173, 224, 229, 249 and 260.

Genevieve Wiseman: pages 19, 77 and 135.

Canadian Living